French Impressions

AF271778

The Dordogne River

from source to sea

George East

A La Puce Publication
www.la-puce.co.uk

Other Books by George East

Home & Dry in France

René & Me

French Letters

French Flea Bites

French Cricket

French Kisses

French Lessons

French Impressions: Brittany

French Impressions: The Loire Valley

Home & Dry in Normandy (compilation)

French Kisses (compilation)

France and the French

Also:

A Year Behind Bars

How to write a Best-Seller

And the Inspector Mowgley Mysteries:

Death Duty

Deadly Tide

Dead Money

LA PUCE PUBLICATIONS

e-mail: lapucepublications@hotmail.co.uk

web site: www.george-east.net

About the Author

If anyone should know his onions about France and the French, it's George East. After he and wife Donella moved to a ruined water mill on ten acres of rivers, woods, meadows and mud in Normandy, George wrote a best-selling series of books about living with the enemy.

The couple then left the Mill of the Flea and moved on to an allegedly haunted manor-house on the vast Lower Normandy marshlands. Their next home was a rambling farmhouse half way up what counts as a mountain in Brittany. Then it was off to a remote hamlet in the Loire Valley.

Since then, the Easts have travelled through and tarried in every one of France's 90-odd departments and 22 regions. This is the third book in the French Impressions series, and George means to continue his sometimes unsteady progress around the country until he runs out of breath - or friends and readers prepared to give him house room.

George East's
French Impressions: The Dordogne River

Published by La Puce Publications

e-mail: lapucepublications@hotmail.co.uk

website: www.george-east.net

ISBN: 978-1-908747-29-7

Typesetting and layout by Nigel Rice

Author's Notes

The clue to what the reader may find in this book comes with the name of the series. The following pages are daubed with my often hasty and probably inaccurate impressions of the places and people encountered while travelling along the Dordogne River. As fans of the 19th-century art movement will tell you, an impression can sometimes give a truer picture than a carefully detailed and studied work.

Sometimes, of course, it can also end up as a bit of a dog's breakfast.

Appreciations

On the technical side, thanks are as usual due to our indefatigable proof reader Sally Moore, Editrix Fran Brooks and designer and tech spec buff Nigel Rice. Thanks and apologies where necessary are also due to all those people whose lives we briefly touched on the road or in bars, restaurants, hotels, bed and breakfast establishments or campsites.

A River Runs Through It

For donkey's years, British Francophiles have been bigging up 'The Dordogne' when they actually mean lots of different places in the heartland of France.

Like Italy's Chiantishire, this part of *France profonde* has long been a favourite destination for holidaying and migrating Brits. Over the years, the borders and realities have blurred and the word 'Dordogne' has been used to evoke a mythical, magical place where the sun always shines, the food and drink is fantastic and the locals forever whimsically quaint.

In fact, though a pretty special place, Dordogne is neither more nor less than a department of the Aquitaine region.

The river of that name rises in the volcanic area of the Auvergne region as the confluence of two embryo waterways, the Dore and the Dogne. In a rather French way, this is not actually how the river got its name, but that need not bother us here.

More certain is that the Dordogne runs from its source on the flank of a dead volcano roughly westwards to where it empties into the sea a tad above Bordeaux.

On the way, it constantly changes direction, size, shape and mood as it passes through six departments and five regions. This means the river and those who follow or use it for any distance pass through a whole clutch of diverse landscapes, climates, cuisine and even languages.

In total, this seemed to me to provide more than enough justification for making the journey and passing on an impression of what we found along the way.

PS. *Before we get started and before anyone writes in to complain about it, we need to have a word about my apparent inconsistency in the use of the definite article when referring to various departments and regions of France. For instance, I call the departments of Dordogne and Lot 'The/the Dordogne' and 'The/the Lot' yet Cantal does not earn the definite article. Nor would I dream of imposing a 'the' on Puy-de-Dôme or Charente-Maritime. Similarly with regions, one normally thinks of The Limousin and The Auvergne, but saying or writing 'The' Aquitaine and 'The' Poitou-Charentes feels clumsy or just plain wrong. I mean, can you imagine someone asking where you went on holiday last year and you replying 'Oh we thought about going to The Normandy, but ending up having a lovely couple of weeks in The Brittany.'? See what I mean? On this side of the Channel, there seems to be no confusion or debate. Regions win a 'the', while counties do not.*

I am told we use 'the' for a number of reasons, including when we know the thing being spoken of ('the moon is very bright tonight') and when there is only one of the objects in that place or surroundings ('we live near the church'). Why the custom with regions and departments of France, I haven't a clue.

So please don't ask me for any justification of this tradition or why I observe it. It is just how it is. It might not seem a big deal to you, but you might be surprised at how many people get really shirty about the use of this normally inoffensive three letter word when talking of specific bits of France.

Some fascinating facts about the River Dordogne

Length: More or less 483 kilometres, or about 300 miles*

Starts at: The Puy de Sancy, Auvergne

Finishes in: The Gironde estuary

Departments passed through on route to the sea:

Puy-de-Dôme

Corrèze

Lot

Dordogne

Gironde (the largest department in Metropolitan France)

Charente-Maritime (the second largest and most populous department)

Regions passed through:

Auvergne

Limousin

Midi-Pyrénées

Aquitaine

Poitou-Charentes

The Dordogne is one of the few rivers (like our own Severn) to have a tidal bore. This does not mean an old sea dog banging on about springs and neap tides, but a rush of water or 'high tide' coinciding conveniently with the water-sporting summer months of July and August.

Because of the meanderings of the river and our frequently going off-piste, the distances I record as having travelled on each leg should not be regarded as remotely accurate or useful. They are no more than a rough guide.

LEG 1

Le Mont-Dore to Mauriac

Distance: 85 kilometres

Region: The Auvergne

Departments: Puy-de-Dôme, Cantal

Puy de Sancy

At first I think the man in the car park is a member of the French Magic Circle, demonstrating his skills to impress fellow motorists.

Then I see he is actually assembling an assortment of travel items, including a collapsible wine rack and what we used to call a hostess trolley from the boot of his tiny Fiat. As he casually produces a sizeable table complete with bench seat, a parasol, wine cooler and condiment rack I realise what is afoot. It is approaching noon, and he is preparing for an informal picnic.

It is a truism disguised as a stereotype that the French take their lunches very seriously, regardless of where they take them. Clearly, this man is merely making sure that the furniture, furnishings, implements and accessories do justice to the spread his wife is working on.

As we pass, I compliment Madame on her breasts as she performs a double mastectomy on a chicken with a casual flick of her Sabatier knife. Being French, she looks at her generous bosom and then the bird, and nods gracious acceptance of the compliment to either or both. Her husband does not pick up on my feeble gag as he is occupied with an extravagant floral table-top display. I am disappointed when he produces the bunch of tiger lilies from the back of the car rather than inside his jacket, but still clap my hands in admiration. He puts the spray of flowers in a vase, then acknowledges my applause with a small and perfectly serious bow.

The car park is full of similarly intricate preparations, and though it is only mid-July and the holiday season is not yet upon us, this indicates that the highest dead volcano in France is a popular attraction.

Taking their name from the Roman god of fire, volcanoes are basically holes in the earth through which liquid rock gushed a very long time ago. They often look like barren and topless mini-mountains or giant, burnt-out firework cones because of the build-up of lava and cinders over aeons. 'Puy' is an old French word for a volcanic hill, and the Châine des Puys stretches for around 50 kilometres in the midst of the great plateau of the Massif Central. The Puy-de-Dôme department is named for the highest volcano in the chain.

Depending on their age and inclinations, the half million visitors who arrive in this part of France every year like to photograph and be photographed, picnic on, climb or even attempt to drive up these sleeping giants.

At 1886 metres, the Puy de Sancy ('mountain of the cross' in ancient Occitan) is the highest point in Central France, topped elsewhere only by the Alps and Pyrénées. It is one of three former volcanoes which make up the satisfyingly street- gang-sounding Mont Dore Massif. It is said the Alps can be seen from the top on a clear day, and during the winter months the slopes of Sancy become a favoured ski slope. Most importantly for our purposes it is also where the Dordogne River first sees the light of day.

The river officially starts its three hundred mile journey to the sea where two springs unite somewhere up the slope. Our self-appointed challenge is to find both sources and log exactly where they become the Dordogne, taking a souvenir sample of the confluence. To be honest, we could just ask in the information office or look at the very big map outside which pinpoints the location of both trickles, but that would seem like cheating.

Instead, we, or rather I, have chosen to fight our way up the south face. I suggest roping ourselves together and taking ice picks and oxygen supplies, but my wife points to a young family pushing a pram and accompanied by a very old lady on double walking sticks high above us on the snowless *piste*.

But before we do the hard bit I suggest we take a ride up to the very top of the mountain. It is my first visit to a ski slope and I have always wanted to travel in the sort of cable car on the roof of which James Bond was often to be found fighting the relevant arch-villain.

Though she has not got a good head for heights, my wife reluctantly agrees. I decide not to tell her about the seventeen passengers killed or seriously injured in an accident here in 1965. Even in France I reckon safety measures must have been tightened up since then.

We labour up the slope to the nearer of the two boarding stations, and find it closed for repairs. This does nothing to reassure my wife, as she points out that if something needs repairing, it must have become broken. This would not be too much of a problem with a washing machine or set of hair straightening tongs, but a breakdown could have more serious implications for people dangling in a small, swaying box hundreds of feet above the ground. This being summertime, she adds gloomily, there is not even any snow to help break the fall.

*   *   *

At the other boarding station, a ragged queue snakes back from the entrance, and most of its constituents look ill-at-ease or even openly agitated. I assume I am picking up on their disquiet, then realise their discomfort is not caused by the prospect of travelling several thousand yards up a mountainside in a flimsy-looking cable-car. It is because they are having to queue before boarding. This is something so contrary to French instinct, nature and social conditioning that the sum of their anxiety is palpable.

Thankfully and before mass hysteria breaks out, one of the two working cars reaches the end of its downward journey, and the queue disintegrates as people surge forward so as to be first on board and gain a favoured position. The action will also gain them the bonus satisfaction of blocking the exit route for disembarking passengers. This love of obstructive behaviour is another very French trait. It is common everywhere that people meet, but best seen in supermarkets where shoppers gain status by the imaginative use of their trolleys to block aisles. Though I am sure it is not true, an embittered British expatriate with permanently lacerated knees once told me there is a popular late night TV programme on *Canal Plus* which is based on our *Supermarket Sweep*. The difference is that rather than rushing round to collect free groceries, the contestants try to stop each other's progress and cause maximum damage and injury on route.

Being in no hurry, we stand back and wait for the scrum to subside.

Finally arriving at the entrance, we find it guarded by a very large man in official costume. He is holding his hand out, and I assume he is expecting a tip. He looks disdainfully down over his huge walrus moustache at my handful of very small change, then points wordlessly at a well-hidden notice which explains that entrance is by ticket only. I ask him where we may get them, and, still without speaking, he points one immaculately oiled and twirled end of his moustache over my shoulder. I turn and see a building cunningly obscured behind a row of snow ploughs and a mountain of as-yet unassembled chair lift components. To be fair, as my wife points out, the word BILLITERIE is written in very large letters above the door.

*   *   *

At the desk, a friendly young lady asks if we want to come back from the top, and I say we would just like to be sure of getting there in one piece. She has the grace not to yawn at hearing a variation of the same line a hundred times a day, smiles and gives us our tickets.

Back at the entrance, the big man with the big moustache is contemplating with deep affection a baguette stuffed with what looks and smells like alternate slices of garlic sausage and goat's cheese in a garlic sauce of minced and puréed garlic with extra garlic dressing. The man and his meal obviously have an assignation which will be consummated in the very near future, and he is indulging in some literally lip-smackingly lubricous foreplay. The sandwich is made up from a whole *gros pain*. This is one of the biggest French loaves and resembles what we would call a family-sized bloomer. In his hand, it looks almost like a dainty bridge roll.

Long aware of the perils of coming between a Frenchman and his food, I smile ingratiatingly and proffer the tickets. The giant murmurs an excuse to his lunch, then he holds a massive hand up to my face, pointing at his wrist with the sharp end of the loaf.

Already suspecting what is afoot, I look at his watch and see that it is seconds away from noon, so our plans for a trip up the mountainside, like the cable car itself, must be put on hold. A surprising number of French businesses still shut at this sacred hour, and I even know of restaurants which close for lunch. Obviously, there will be no more rides up to the top of the volcano for at least a couple of hours.

Before we make our way down the slope to find somewhere to while away the time by eating and drinking too much, I say I hope the cable car got to the top before noon, or the passengers would have had to stay in suspense until the end of the lunch break. The attendant again smiles apologetically at his baguette, then looks up at the distant car, which is moored at the docking station above. He does not speak but looks thoughtful, and I hope for the sake of future travellers that I have not put any ideas into his head.

*   *   *

We have eaten very well at a nearby village, and the food as well as our surroundings seemed somehow more alpine than French.

Though we are in the middle of France, the wooden, chalet-style houses and sloping green unfenced fields surrounding the base of the dead volcano suggest we might be in Sound of Music territory rather than a prime French bottled-water zone. Stretching into the far distance, green and pleasant hills are dotted with cows and mountain goats, some even having bells around their necks. As there does not seem to be too many places where they could get lost in this most open of terrains, I wonder if the bells are to keep the tourists happy.

Eagles dare overhead, and, in spite of the time of year, ribbons of smoke curl from wooden chalets into an untroubled and almost painfully blue sky, Most things to do with nature here seem on a grand scale, and green is the predominant colour.

As I navigate a hairpin bend and try to get round the corner before a giant Euro-lorry forces us through the barrier and into the abyss, I reflect on just how varied the different parts of this great country can be, even if driving standards and attitudes are constant.

*   *   *

Back at the boarding station, a ragged queue has formed, but those in it look much less ill-at-ease. Clearly, they have all had a good lunch. At the gate, our silent giant has been replaced by a very voluble small man with a walkie-talkie radio-receiver strapped to his hip. As he is equipped with this most prized of status symbols, he must be senior to the giant bouncer. As any frequent visitor to French tourist attractions will know, the walkie-talkie is similar to an officer's swagger stick in symbolic rather than actual function. Replaced in usefulness by the mobile phone, it may have a flat battery or not even be switched on, but it bestows and denotes authority, and shows the bearer is empowered to boss people around at a distance as well as close to hand.

After a lengthy wait for no apparent reason - par for the course in most tourist attractions anywhere in the world - we shuffle forward and I pass our tickets to the new guardian at the gate. He looks at them and then at me as if surprised, then nods to a platform where steps lead up to the gondola. It looks smaller and much more frail at close quarters. It also appears full, but pressure from the queue behind forces us up and into the glass and metal lozenge.

Although we have not yet taken off it is swinging quite markedly, and from the inside appears to be made of much more glass than metal. Obviously, the organisers are making up for the loss of the car under repair by filling this one to and beyond capacity.

After a deal of pushing and shoving, we find ourselves in a corner, noses to the glass. Just when I think no more people can possibly be forced in, the whole vehicle tips alarmingly as the man mountain and his moustache squeeze through the door. Thankfully he has consumed his oversized sandwich. A ripple of nervous laughter runs through the car as the giant cleaves a path through the pack and begins directing individuals to move to different parts of the cabin. He is obviously trimming the vessel before we set sail.

Either because he has not taken a shine to me or more likely because I am obviously the second heaviest person on the premises, I am detailed to go and stand in the opposite corner to him. I note that he is orchestrating our movements by waving a walkie-talkie like the one we saw on the hip of the small man at the door. Either there are two units, the big man has suddenly been promoted above the small one, or was still hungry after lunch and has eaten his rival.

As the passengers are shunted around, I note that the conductor is keeping an eye on a strange device at the business end of the car. Its main constituent is a brass pointer, with the tip swaying back and forth along a curved and calibrated scale. At either end of the scale is a red section. I ask the *conducteur* about it, and he tersely explains that the needle indicates both the wind velocity and the angle at which the cabin is hanging. If the needle reaches and stays in the red, we will not be taking off.

Eventually, the swingometer and the driver are satisfied, and he throws a switch and presses various buttons. It is all very much like a scene from a stage production of *The Time Machine*. For a moment, nothing happens, then we all stagger forward as the cabin lurches backwards before moving up and away from the platform. We rise steadily on the wings of a collective sigh of relief, and it is a strange sensation to be moving through thin air so slowly and at such an angle.

But not all of us are enjoying the journey. With her back to the window and eyes tightly shut, my wife is holding me more closely than I can remember since the early days of our relationship.

Many people think that the name for a fear of heights is vertigo, but that word refers to a sensation of dizziness which can sometimes result from looking down from a high place. Sometimes also confused with agoraphobia (related to a fear of open spaces), acrophobia or a morbid fear of heights is believed to be the most common of phobias. A phobia is technically an irrational or abnormal fear, but I cannot see that being afraid of the consequences of falling from a great height could be described as irrational. A glance between my feet and through the glass floor of the gondola confirms the increasing distance between us and the ground.

It is a shame my wife is not enjoying the ride, as our position gives a unique perspective of the glorious scenery. From this angle and height, the undulating and far-reaching landscape of green seems to stretch forever below an upturned bowl of pure, uninterrupted blue.

Our slow and silent progress continues, and my wife only opens her eyes when I tell her we are within jumping distance of the disembarking platform. Then, like a horse refusing a jump, the car lurches, dips, swings wildly from side to side then stops dead.

There is a chorus of screams and shouts, amongst which I seem to recognise my own voice, but an octave higher than usual. Then a grim silence falls, broken only by a creaking noise and the whistle of the wind blowing through the cable wires.

In a suspense movie, this would be when a rasping twanging noise indicates that the strands of the main support cable are beginning to part. In our real-life drama, the driver talks very quickly on his walkie-talkie while several passengers flout the strict laws by lighting up. I note that none of the non-smokers complains or attempts to open a window, and I consider asking the sweating man next to me for a drag on his roll-up.

As I think about breaking my three-year abstinence from the weed, the car lurches again. There is a hum from the control box, and we start moving again. I am relieved to note that we are moving in an upwards direction.

We dock, and there is a more than usually frenetic scrum to be the first on to the landing platform. Departing completely from the norm, the people waiting to travel back down are making no attempt to push their way on board before we get off. Also unsurprisingly, no explanation or apology is given for the heart-stopping interlude when the cable car came up short of its destination.

As I help my wife out on to the platform and she tries not to look down through the gap between car and ramp, I recall a statistic concerning the French and how few of them leave the ground. It is a matter of record that eighty six percent of French people have never flown.

Previously, I had thought this was because they felt no need to visit far-flung and exotic lands on holiday with so much choice at home. Now I think their reluctance may be because they have travelled in a dodgy cable car.

*   *   *

Today is clearly a day for first-time experiences.

I have never before journeyed in a cable car, and this is the first time I have travelled down a ski slope without skis or snow.

We are safely back in the car park after a winding trek over more than a mile of scree, which makes walking downhill in desert boots quite challenging. The reason we decided to descend by foot was officially because I had mistakenly only bought us one-way tickets to the top. In truth, I think we both preferred the slow slog downhill to the prospect of using the cable car to get back to where we started. The benefits of taking the hard way down included working up an appetite for dinner, seeing some interesting high-altitude vegetation, and finding and posing for snaps beside what I hope is the source of the Dordogne river.

As we pass the little Fiat, I see that the temporary dining room has been conjured back into the boot, and the magician and his wife are taking their ease in a pair of camping chairs. He is looking very serious and studying what I take to be a newspaper, so I assume he must be catching on up the latest bad news of the severe financial mess France is in. As we draw closer, however, I see that what is absorbing his total concentration is the dinner menu for the restaurant at the exit to the car park.

I wish him success, and am relieved to see that things are very much back to normal and down-to-earth.

Wet, Wet, Wet

The Massif Central is officially the wettest place in France. This is partly due to it being a meeting place for clouds from the cold Atlantic and warm air from the Mediterranean. In the dampest parts, more than two metres of water can fall from the skies in a year. This is good news for those companies which make a fortune bottling and selling water.

Put basically, mineral water is the result of a never-ending natural cycle. It is spooky to think that virtually every drop of water on the planet has gone through the process of falling from the sky as rain before evaporating back into the atmosphere. As it rises, the evaporated water forms rain clouds and so it goes on and on.

Part of what makes mineral water so special and costly is that it spends much longer in the water cycle. On its journey it takes a detour through the aquifer (permeable rock beneath the surface of the earth) before emerging through natural or artificial sources. Depending on the geology through which it has passed, the water will have gathered a number of minerals. To qualify for the top title and price potential, any mineral water has to conform to a concentration level set by the World Health Organisation.

Another pretty obvious requirement is that the water is not contaminated by agricultural or human waste products. The volcanic deposits insulating the sources in this part of France provide a perfect shield, and by the time the water has worked its way back to the surface, the only additions will have been the very welcome minerals of calcium, potassium, bromine, sodium, bicarbonate and or fluoride.

Sniffy Francophobes allege that the French got a liking for bottled water because the stuff coming out of their taps was undrinkable. That is partly true, but although France has some of the cleanest tap water in the world nowadays, the Gallic enthusiasm for mineral water is unabated. Year on year, the consumption of tap water goes down, and more than a quarter of French people say they never drink it.

Sixty-four percent say they drink mineral water at least once a week. In fact, only one percent of all domestic (tap) water produced in France is used for drinking.

Based on those figures, it means a lot of French people only imbibe any form of domestic water in their coffee, and rely on the bottled stuff and other liquids to slake their thirsts.

On average, every French adult drinks around a hundred litres of still or fizzy mineral water a year, and France is second only to Italy in consumption terms. These staggering stats also help explain why the only form of litter consistently seen in any part of France is the empty mineral water bottle.

As an example of the level of production achievable, the local S.M.D.A. (Sources du Mont Dore et Auvergne) belongs to the giant Danone organisation, and is the company responsible for the Evian and Volvic brands. SMDA exploits the three main Mont Dore springs, and just one hundred employees knocked out a third of a billion litres of bottled water in 2005, the most recent year for which figures are available.

Perhaps to the regret of mineral water makers, it does not rain all the time in the Auvergne. But given the precipitation statistics it was perhaps not a good idea to choose to spend a night in the open at a point not much lower than the summit of the Puy de Sancy.

The thing I find about camping is that it is even more dependent on the weather than cricket. If the sun shines, it is one of life's pleasures to bask lizard-like with glass in hand beside your tent while pretending to be roughing it.

On the other hand, few things I have experienced are less pleasurable than laying on a sloping piece of land beneath a sheet of leaky plastic as muddy water flows in one end of your sleeping bag and out the other.

In my childhood, we camped so much because it was all the family could afford in the way of a holiday. The joke was how we went home and told everyone how much we enjoyed it.

In those more spartan days, the essential point of camping was getting near to nature. Now, the objective seems to be to keep it at bay and recreate the environment and gadgets you left behind at home. A lot of tents seem better appointed and even roomier than the houses in which some people grew up a few decades ago.

I find it interesting how a visit to a campsite can also demonstrate basic cultural characteristics. As it is the French who like to make a big deal of a picnic, it is the Germans and Dutch who go overboard when camping or caravanning. After years of observation, I can differentiate between the races without having to look at their car licence plates. Generally, Dutch pitches will have been made to look neat and yet homely, and strapped to the back of their campers will often be a couple of classic canal-side sit-up-and-beg bicycles with baskets on the front, ready for the owners to pedal into town for provisions.

Dutch tents will invariably be of the lofty standing-room variety. This may be no more than a practical consideration, as I have yet to meet a Dutch man or woman on a campsite that I did not have to look up to. Often, little gardens will have been created with neat lines of knee-high white plastic fencing. So far I have not seen any tulips or a miniature windmill, and I think the displays are made as much to please the eye of passers-by as to mark out territorial boundaries.

On the other hand, the thing about Germans laying out towels at poolside to claim territory has its equivalent at most European campsites. The one we are staying at tonight is sparsely populated but gives a perfect example of cultural differentials.

Near the entrance, a French caravan had been apparently abandoned, and is almost blocking all access to the rest of the site. Beyond that, a Munich-licensed camper had created a no-go area by winding the sort of brightly marked tape you see at murder scenes around the trees surrounding that corner of the site. We will not set up camp beside his foreboding campervan as I fear we might wake up in the morning and find our pitch has been annexed.

*   *   *

An hour later and it is difficult to see our neighbours as we are surrounded by a thick and clammy wall of white. I suggest it is mist, but my wife says it is not-so low cloud, and that she hopes we are not on the flight path to Clermont-Ferrand airport.

*   *   *

Early morning, and we are heading for the nearest town to find a hotel room in which to dry out and sleep for more than twenty consecutive minutes.

The rain started as I pushed the last tent peg in, and persevered until I pulled it out again. In between, we had a spectacularly sleepless night caused by leaks from above and below.

Our ancient tent was no match for the downpour, and worse, the inflatable mattress sprang a leak. It took around an hour for us to reach ground level, and those who know will agree that a partially inflated airbed is more uncomfortable than a totally deflated one. After see-sawing about while trying to trim our prone positions by re-positioning our bodies and adding and subtracting rucksacks and other weights, I gave up and reached for the foot pump.

It is one of those all-rubber affairs with a dome-shaped bit on which to jump up and down. From it a length of tubing leads, with a selection of adaptors to suit the size of the inlet valve on the mattress. We long ago lost the correct adaptor, and the only one which fits is too small. This means that for every stamp of the foot, half the air which should have gone into the mattress escapes through the gap around the adaptor. Because of this shortcoming, the pumper also needs to adopt a crouched position during the operation. Being cocooned in a sodden sleeping bag in the

(25)

middle of the night did not make the operation any easier, and there was another problem.

The necessarily jerky action makes the pump squeak like a tortured mouse, and the escaping air wheezes like a 40 fags-a-day man coming to the final stages of the London Marathon. What my silhouette looked like through the thin canvas wall of the tent as I rose up and down over the mattress with my own gasping matching that of the air pump is anybody's guess.

When we checked out in the morning, the campsite manager observed dryly that I must be tired, as the owner of the German camper had complained about the grunts and squeaks and gasps coming from our tent throughout the night. When I asked about the French couple on the other side, the manager said the male half had mentioned the noise in an admiring way, and said it had changed his mind completely about the English and their attitude to sex.

Le Mont-Dore

As with people, I find some towns immediately appealing or not, and often for no obvious reason. I don't think I would want to spend the rest of my life in Le Mont-Dore, but I'd gladly drop by to say hello when passing.

Just up the road from the ski centre of Sancy, the town looks like it makes a nice living from the people who choose to spend some part of their life whizzing down the slopes of a dead volcano.

The surrounding area is not short on *pistes*, and offers 45 kilometres of downhill runs, plus another twenty-five of cross country treks. Thus the no-nonsense, cheerful little town has a long history of catering for well-heeled visitors, and the number of designer shops and the cost of the goods in them shows they know their market well.

The skiers are actually relatively recent visitors, having replaced the prosperous but constantly indisposed people (which France seems full of) who since Roman Times would flock to immerse themselves in the town's wonderfully over-the-top bath house.

As the thermal springs feeding the baths contain bicarbonate of soda and arsenic, it comes as a surprise that the punters like to drink as well as sit in the waters. Probably to justify the treatment fee, all the thermal bath houses in this part of France look like a cross between an over-the-top1970s bingo hall and a Byzantine knocking shop.

Originally known as Mont-Dore-les-Bains for obvious reasons, the bathhouses were serviced by twelve thermal springs, and specialized in the treatment and alleged cure of many ailments, including bronchitis, TB, Asthma and rheumatics. Nobody enjoys ill-health more than the French, and it has been so for a long time. Roman baths relics can be seen in the town park, and famous visitors who came to take the waters included the Duchesse de Berry, who led a failed insurrection against Louis-Philippe in the Vendee.

But the main reason I found Le Mont-Dore so attractive may be because it is home to a real cracker of a bar. That's always a very positive and persuasive point when I am recalling or reviewing a town. This one seemed full of character and characters and somehow seems out of time and as if it belongs to a past that perhaps never was. Sadly I shall never be able to call in at Gauguin, Van Gogh and Toulouse Lautrec's locals in Paris, but I reckon this one is exactly the sort they would use.

The single room is large, but crowded with interesting people and things. Under a collection of mismatching carpet squares, the floor is laid with obviously original hand-made tiles which would fetch a literally breath-taking price in the Fulham branch of the We Saw You Coming Antique Emporium. On them sit a dozen Egyptian-themed original art deco tables which would probably fetch enough money in any London auction room for the bar owner to shut up shop and retire.

Hanging from a wall is a hugely framed mirror doubling as a menu board. Details of the dish of the day and other special offers have been written on the glass in what looks like period whitewash. The price of the midday special of *cassoulet* and complimentary bottle of wine is also pleasingly old-fashioned.

Two of the other walls are thickly lined with back-and-white photographs of Parisian scenes and household names of the increasingly distant past. Yves Montand and Alain Delon are frozen for ever at their most cockily handsome. Alongside them, Edith Piaf stares owlishly at the camera, and below her is a line-up of some of the most seriously talented and acclaimed French jazz stars of the pre and post-War years. Continuing the theme, a battered upright piano in the corner is obviously there for work and not merely show.

But the crowning glory is what must be one of the very few surviving original zinc bar counters in all France. Once upon a time, thousands of Parisian drinking haunts boasted these chest-high, metal-topped counters for which they were named. Nowadays and like stand-to-deliver toilets, the zinc bar is making a comeback in trendy locations, but this one is clearly the real thing. Just to make it absolutely right, on the bar is a period help-yourself-hard-boiled egg rack. On the wall behind the bar there are no optics, but proper chromium pourers in the necks of dozens of interesting-looking bottles.

Also in exact keeping with her surroundings is the owner of the bar. Madame's taste and status is obvious from the quality and understated style of her dress and jewellery. The lady of the house is of about the same vintage as the art-deco furniture, but her face is so strongly planed in cheekbone and jaw line that it seems unlined.

Seeing my admiring stare, Madame glides along the bar towards us, and I am tempted to lean over and see if she is on castors rather than feet. I make our order and we take a seat to drink in the action.

Above us, the ceiling is an inimitable shade of old gold, brought about only by the smoke of a million cigarettes. Sadly, those days are gone, and the dwindling number of French smokers are forced to sit outside. It is still raining, but I am pleased to see a hardy trio are taking part in a smoking competition. This is another disappearing French art form.

The coterie at the wrought-iron table beneath the awning have very different smoking styles, but are surprisingly similar in appearance. They do not appear to be related, but obviously share interests and philosophies. Each is expressing his bohemian sensibilities with carefully distressed leather trousers and waistcoat over collarless shirts. Each is wearing a fedora hat from which dangles the sort of grey and lank pony tail nurtured by men who wish to make up for what they have lost from the top of their heads.

One is artfully smoking what looks and smells even from a distance like an unfiltered *Disque Bleu*. Another is examining the glowing end of a small cigar, while the third member of the group wields an unfeasibly large hand-rolled cigarette which probably contains more than just tobacco.

The *Disque Bleu* man favours the Yves Montand approach, with cigarette dangling precariously from his lower lip. The small cigar man is using his stogie to punctuate his animated discourse, while the man with the monster roll-up needs both hands to support it.

As we watch the show, a man in chef's whites emerges from an alleyway next to the restaurant across the street to join in the group discussion. He favours the 1940s movie Parisian private detective style, extracting a cigarette from his tunic and inserting it into the corner of his mouth with one hand, while the other produces, snaps open and ignites a Zippo lighter in one smooth motion.

Seeing her new customer, Madame glides from behind the bar, and I see the label of the bottle she carries bears an illustration of a green fairy. Now I know we are in for an interesting evening, as what is in the bottle was almost synonymous with the classic Parisian zinc bar.

Absinthe is or was an anise-flavoured drink much favoured by 19th-century Paris-based artists and literary luminaries. Later artistic big hitters who were on intimate terms with the Green Fairy included Oscar Wilde and Ernest Hemmingway. A favoured way of drinking it was from the glass but via a sugar lump, Absinthe is actually no stronger or less strong than many spirits, but has been credited with sending its habitués blind, mad or both. Such was the power of perception over reality, that the Green Fairy was banned in France in 1915.

Whatever its strength, Absinthe, like the smell of Disque Bleu and the Paris Metro makes my heart fonder for all things French. As Madame returns from the terrace, I invite her to leave the bottle at our table, and bring a glass for herself if she can spare a little while to tell us of her splendid bar's history.

She graciously agrees, and as I reach for a spare chair, someone strikes up on the piano. The tune is a between-wars jazz classic, and the atmosphere it generates lacks only a fug of cigarette smoke. Outside, it is still raining, and I am glad it is. Had it not started we would be under canvas rather than inside this delightful bar, and I know where I would rather be in any weather.

Le Mont-Dore to St Nectaire

I am negotiating a hangover as well as the steep and winding road which will take us westward on the trail of the Dordogne river. We had intended to seek out the Grand Cascade, a waterfall which is one of the area's major attractions, but feel we have seen enough of falling water for a while.

The road out of the town flanks a sheer drop, and the potential for near or even actual death experiences means most of the French motorists using it will be driving with even more suicidal abandon than usual.

Rounding a hairpin bend, we come across a breakdown truck and I brake sharply to avoid skidding through a ragged gap in the crash barrier and providing the truck's owner with some extra income. I fleetingly consider that this is why it is parked in such a mad place, then see the vehicle is already working.

Pulling over, I get out and peer over the edge and see that the truck's winch wire trails down the steep, tree-lined slope to where an upturned car has come to rest against a mortally damaged pine. On the road, a group of men in high-visibility jackets and hard hats are busily lighting each other's cigarettes and snarling up the traffic flow by showing green and red flags at the same time at each end of the single lane between the lorry and the rock face of the mountain.

Another couple of workers are on an official smoke break by the crumpled barrier and giving advice to a man abseiling down the slope. I note he is the only one not wearing a hard hat, then realise he is one of the pony-tailed trio from the terrace of the bar last night. I recognise him not only by his hairstyle, but the way he is holding his cigarette with what he obviously considers to be his spare hand.

As we squeeze past the truck I see that the owner of the bar is sitting in an old Peugeot shooting brake parked alongside the barrier. Next to her is another of the trio of smokists from last evening. She looks concerned, and our eyes meet as we pass although there is no sign of recognition.

Escaping from the bottleneck I consider the possibilities of the tableau. Perhaps the owner of the upturned car is the third member of the artful smokers group, and the man abseiling down the slope was ignoring the health and safety regulations to rescue him. Or perhaps it is his car and he is intent on saving on what would obviously be substantial recovery costs. It might even be that the stricken car belongs to owner of the bar, and her customers are helping her out.

An impatient toot from a lorry trying to attach itself to my rear bumper jars me from my reverie and I speed up and away from the mystery. I will never know who owns the car at the bottom of the ravine, how it came to be there and whether or not the driver is still inside. Or, if so, is badly injured or even still alive, This lack of closure is both the good and bad thing about making fleeting contacts and observations while travelling through France and other people's lives.

*　　*　　*

This is a truly remarkable part of a remarkably landscaped country.

In the French way, there were no warning signs as we approached the breakdown truck, but there was a diversion sign at the crossroads at the top of the steep climb. The fact that the diversion is *after* the event it is meant to be diverting traffic from is quite normal in our experience.

For once I am grateful for the whims of the diverters, as had we taken the direct route to our destination we would have missed a really dramatic panorama. A roadside sign informs us we are in the land of lakes and volcanoes, and it is, like the diversion, unnecessary. The great blue dome of the sky is starkly pierced by volcanoes and granite outcrops, and in between are the mirrored surfaces of great lakes. There is no sense or sign of human habitation, and we could be time travellers venturing into an ancient world.

At 400 hundred square kilometres, *Le Parc Naturel Régional des Volcans d'Auvergne* is the largest in the country, and the sheer scale makes the word 'park' seem a bit of an understatement. Once this place would have been the haunt of mammoths and mastodons; over the eons, dinosaurs have mutated into the two hundred species of birds which call this place home.

Raptors competing to make a living here include royal and black kite, kestrels and peregrines, harriers and ospreys. On the ground, otters are common, and even Atlantic salmon besport themselves in the Allier river before making off to open waters via the Loire.

As we devour this feast of nature, a pair of Golden Eagles appear high above. Then, as if they have seen us and are curious, they plummet down to investigate.

As with humans, the male is the show-off, and the larger bird is performing increasingly more daring and impressive aerobatic feats. Surely, I say to my wife, he is trying to impress us or his mate, or is in the pay of the Massif Central tourist authority.

When he swoops down in an apparently suicidal dive, I see that his wingspan is easily wider than our car. In fact, he comes so close that if I were quick enough I could reach out and fleetingly touch this lord of the air. Then he is gone and we are left breathless by the sheer majesty of the spectacle and his lordly insouciance.

For thousands of generations, mankind has marvelled at birds in flight and dreamed of following them into the sky. I raise a hand in salute, and fanciful though I am being, it seems to me that the great bird ducks its wings in haughty response before soaring up and away towards the far horizon.

St Nectaire

To give him his Sunday-best title, Saint Nectarius of Auvergne is said to have been the first evangelist to set foot in this part of France. He suffered a particularly nasty martyrdom and was thought highly enough of to have not only a town but also a cheese named for him.

In France and even with a cheese for every day of the year to name, this counts as a real honour. The town has and upper and lower part, with the commercial centre sited suitably in the lower part, whilst the church looks disdainfully down from Haute St Nectaire.

Before making the climb, we pool our cash to buy a sliver of the eponymous cheese from the grocery store by the car park. We find the owner busy with a coach load of eager customers, and looking at the price per kilo I doubt he would have been able to cut a slice thin enough to meet our budget.

For many tourists, a church is a church, and something to be necessarily ticked off before leaving an ancient town. I find nearly all old churches interesting, especially those which have changed little down the ages. Like pubs, an ancient church links us to the past, has its own character and ambience, and the best seem to hold the past within their walls.

This one certainly has a long provenance of spirituality, as it stands on the site of a temple devoted to Apollo. Neither the press of tourists in their violently coloured anoraks nor the recorded Gregorian plainchant issuing from hidden loudspeakers diminishes the atmosphere. Standing in front of the altar and in spite of the distractions I can smell the incense and hear the devotions of congregations long dead.

One of the reasons for the atmosphere and the throng may be that this place has more than a whiff of *Da Vinci Code* allure to it.

The church is said to hold the secret of where a vast

treasure is buried nearby, and has the added mythological status of a dragon guarding the hoard. Adding to the menu of myth and legend, somewhere beneath the church is the entrance to a magical grotto where the waters turn all they touch into stone.

I think the real treasure is closer to home, as the tourists are queuing up to put two Euro pieces into a slot machine in return for a St. Nectaire medallion. Elsewhere are other bargain buys. Nearby is a cabinet containing busts and statuettes of the great man, including a copy of his arm. A guide tells me that the original relic is kept on the premises, but not for sale.

Murol

Like cures for baldness or devices promising to increase the size of one's privatest of parts, many French markets do not live up to hopes and expectations.

The typical small-town, rain-swept French square holding a handful of stallholders intent on making any customers as unhappy as they are inevitably falls short of the popular image. This is a more than common sight in the north of the country in the winter months.

Perhaps for no other reason than where it is, Murol market could have sprung into life from the pages of a holiday brochure or a Peter Mayle book. It is also a classic example of French organisational thinking.

Arriving with the sun, we find the market clearly popular. There are dozens of stalls and hundreds of visitors. Being British, we assume that the area of narrow cobbled streets which the traders and their stalls occupy will have been pedestrianised for the duration of the market.

We realise this is probably not the case as a battered Mercedes comes charging towards us, scattering shoppers and even stallholders in all directions. In Britain there would have been considerable antipathy and a good chance of a punch-up. Here, none of the pedestrians makes a complaint or even scowls at the driver, who is a portly red-faced middle-aged man who would be a shoo-in for Mr Toad in any production of *Wind in the Willows*.

As he whizzes past I extricate myself from a display on a tripe stall, shake my fist and mouth a selection of suitable Anglo-Saxon suggestions. He merely gives a grade five Gallic shoulder shrug and looks at me as if I am mad as he aims for an old lady resting on her Zimmer frame.

After paying for the tripe clinging to my jacket, we make our way along the rows of stalls. The goods on offer and how they are priced are another fine demonstration of cultural differentials. In Britain we like to think that the market is the place to go to buy things cheaper than they would be priced in shops. In France, the opposite applies. People actually come to market prepared or actually keen to pay more for a handful of bananas or a loaf of bread. Somehow, being bought in the open air directly from a human being adds to the status and thus the price. There is also the food snob bonus of being seen to be paying top dollar for goods which must be fresher or better than could be had in the local superstore.

At the Murol market, there is actually an air of an auction taking place, with customers competing to secure the limited supply of certain goods. This is because it is summertime and there are many tourists amongst the locals. The syndrome is most evident at the cheese stall. Murol is yet another town with a cheese named for it, and it is a sort of younger brother of St Nectaire. This gives the cheese stall here top status, and it is under siege. Most aggressive and careless with their money are the obvious tourists, and we watch a scrimmage of puce-faced men with ill-advised shorts waving large denomination notes to show they mean business. Two look ready to come to blows over a wodge of Roquefort which they could buy at half the price at the nearby Carrefour supermarket.

Next to the cheese stall, a man in a suit is sitting at a table bearing the logo of the Credit Agricole bank. There is a surprisingly orderly queue waiting to be interviewed, and I suspect they are seeking mortgages to enable them to buy a man-sized slice of St Nectaire.

Further on we stop at a stall selling what we would call clogs. The old French word *galoche* is where we get 'galoshes' from when talking about rubber overshoes. For some reason, that is also what a particular brand of surface-to-air anti-ballistic missile is known as in Russia. To make things even more complicated, *galoche* is also slang for what we would call a French kiss. Having said that, however, nowadays the younger and cooler French person is most likely to call a French kiss a French kiss. This trend has not pleased those who try to defend the language against English invasion.

The wooden-soled *galoche* has a rubber upper, and as an overshoe became known as a galosh in Britain from around the Middle Ages. The stall is not doing much business, and this may be because of the breath-taking price of the footwear but more likely the somewhat off-putting appearance of the stallholder. If the manic car driver looked like Mr Toad, this man could have stepped from the pages of any Scandinavian fairy tale featuring trolls. He is short and stocky, with a deep chest and wide shoulders. From a grizzled spade-shaped grey beard, exceptionally big ears and nose protrude. I cannot see his feet, but I would bet they are also oversize and would have to be to act as a counterpoint to his massive upper body, especially if there were a strong wind to which his ears were exposed. I hear him talking to his partner, a woman remarkably similar in appearance but with a much less bushy beard, and it is definitely not a form of French I have heard before. Then I see a sign on the stall and realise the couple are Basque.

Like the structure and roots of their language, the origins of the Basque race is a mystery. Their homelands straddle the border between France and Spain and they are a truly ancient race. The word 'sabotage' comes from protesters throwing a *sabot* rather than a spanner into the works, but I do not know the connection between the Basques and the sexily supportive female undergarment. The only other Basque word I know is 'bizar', which, quite bizarrely, means 'beard'.

Our eyes meet and he smiles, tweaks his beard and nods at mine as if to identify our bond in a generally beardless society. Then he looks down at my feet before reaching for a large pair of galoshes. I smile weakly, but am lost. As well as being good at shoemaking, Basque salesmen are obviously good at spotting a sucker.

*   *   *

France is full of castles, but many of what the French call *châteaux* are usually no more than very big houses with lots of spires, towers and other twiddly bits. Here in the Puy-de-Dôme department we are in proper *châteaux-fort* territory, where a castle is a castle, or as we might also say, a fort.

For sure, the word 'foreboding' could have been invented to describe the brooding castle high above Murol. Its first incarnation was in the 12th century, when it was built on a basalt outcrop to keep an eye on several important routes though the liege lord's territory. It was jazzed-up over the years and became an even more intimidating and impregnable fortress. In the years of the Revolution it was a bandit's hideout, then a prison before falling into ruin in the 19th century. It is still an awesome sight, and I think Guy de Maupassant got it just right when he gave his first impressions in 1885:

'It astonishes the eye more than any other ruin by its simple mass, its majesty, its grave and imposing air of majesty. It stands there, alone, high as a mountain, a dead queen, but still the queen of the valleys stretched out beneath it.'

Lake Chambon

Someone said that all lakes are the same but a bit different. I suppose he or she meant that they are all, at the end of day, just holes in the ground which have been filled with water.

We have walked around, swam in and boated on hundreds of lakes in France, and I take the critic's point. Most will have a story, but they have often been dreamed up to make the place seem more interesting.

There is one in Brittany which is said to mask the gates of Hell, and many preside over buried treasures and whole drowned villages. The true back-story about Lake Chambon is that it was formed around 30,000 years ago when one of the newer volcanoes - the Puy de Tartaret - first erupted. The convulsions caused a huge landslide which in turn formed a dam which created the lake. It is a good size at nearly 150 acres (60 hectares), but at only 15 metres (less than ten fathoms) at its deepest point it is more of a giant puddle than a lake.

When we arrive, the main attraction to a group of elderly English tourists is not the lake, but an obviously brand new automatic public toilet which has been erected on the shore.

The shiny cubicle has a door as flush and tightly fitting as the entry to an air-lock on a space ship, and a panel beside it is covered with buttons and lights and dials. Being a French installation, there is no information in any language with regard to which button does what.

As the boldest of the men in the party tentatively prods at the buttons in random order, a man in official overalls approaches with a determined step. A general sigh of relief goes up and some of the ladies begin to uncross their legs. Obviously, relief is at hand.

As we watch expectantly, he marches to the back of the cubicle and disappears. We wait for a long moment, but when nothing whirrs or flashes or makes any other Dr Who-type noises I walk round to investigate. The man has been doing what all French men like to do in public, and has reached the shaking stage. He then nods affably at me as he zips up and strides back towards his van.

I ask him if he knows how to operate the machine, but he gives the universal Gallic shrug and says we will have to go to the town hall. I ask if that is where the instructions are kept, and he says no, but there is a toilet there they might let the ladies use.

La Bourboule

If there is a place where old hotels go to die, La Bourboule must be strongly in the running. Going by the average age of the residents, not a few people must also choose to end their days here.

Once upon a time, La Bourboule was a very swish place, but times and tastes change. The population of the town has halved since 1930, which gives an indication of when things began to go downhill. Or rather, not downhill.

Nowadays and in an apparent effort to re-invent itself for modern tastes, it bills itself as a ski resort. This is a bit of a liberty as there are no ski-slopes at La Bourboule. There is, though, a *telecabine* (cable car) which goes up to the Plateau de Charlannes 1300 feet above the town. A half mile to the west, a small dam across the Dordogne has created a picturesque lake. All in all, this is a pleasant part of the river's progress westward.

There is not a jogger in sight when we bowl into town, but a few elderly people are taking a promenade, or at least putting one foot in front of the other. Earlier, I noticed a prominent notice by the town boundary sign which read STATION OXYGENE. If it marks a supply site, this probably gives a further clue about the age and condition of many of the residents.

We roll along the main street and it soon becomes clear that the town is almost a stereotype. It is obviously a place of faded splendour where wealthy French and English people of a certain age would come to take the air and the waters, eat very well and have a punt at the Casino. The anglicised names of many of the former hotels lining the main street are still vaguely visible on the upper storeys, and Grands and Supremes abound. Eerily, most of the soaring frontages house shops, cafes and bars at street level, but have been abandoned to time and nature from the first floor up. It is disconcerting to see a smart *boulangerie* at eye level, and above it a gaunt, peeling frontage with empty eye-sockets instead of windows. It makes the names in faded lettering a poignant reminder of the good old days. It is also a reminder of how all things die, and how great empires, dynasties and even the grandest of hotels come to the end of their days.

*   *   *

There is something decidedly English about the park at la Bourboule. It is all very neat and symmetrical, with exceptionally well-tended lawns. There are winding paths, a boating lake and even a miniature train which leads to the telecabine station. The parc Fenêstre also boasts a vegetable garden, and it is growing the first runner beans I have seen in France. Being in a posh health spa, the rods up which the tendrils crawl are of ornately-fashioned silver metal rather than common bamboo.

We walk through the gardens to the cable car station and - much to my wife's relief - find that it is out of action. A very nice man in overalls takes the trouble to climb down from the top of the gondola and apologise for our wasted journey; he even offers us a free ride if we return when the season begins.

After meeting the affable man we encounter a very rude woman. The difference and perhaps the reason for her hostility is that she works in the tourist office.

The *bureau de tourisme* is housed in the town hall. The gingerbread and gilt building is almost as grandly over-the-top as the casino and spa baths, but there is certainly no welcome mat at the entrance. As we enter, the immaculately coiffed and made-up but severe looking young woman looks up from her computer, scowls, then returns to her work. Frozen out, we look through the hundreds of brochures and pamphlets but can find none in English.

Eventually I stand at the desk and clear my throat with increasing volume until the young woman looks up. Having established that she cannot or will not speak my language, I say we cannot find any brochures in English. Her lip curls

(44)

and she says that they are in French as we are in France. I accept this as a reasonable point, but mention that several million foreigners who cannot speak the language of God do visit her country every year. In fact, I say, I have heard that La Bourboule has long been known as the English Town.

The woman's eyes flash, then she gives a silky smile, parts her blood-red lips and says with deep satisfaction, 'Pas encore, monsieur, pas encore...'

*   *   *

I think it worth mentioning at this point that it is still not unusual to find a French tourist office where the only language spoken is French. This is not so much because of xenophobia but just because that's how it's always been. It is a tradition many French tourist and holiday venues like to maintain.

Although France is the most visited country on earth, all tourist notices and information and services seemed aimed very primarily at the natives. This is because ninety percent of French people holiday at home. It is also because the French know just what a beautiful and attractive country they have, and believe we should all be grateful for being allowed to visit and spend lots of money there.

Things are changing and my initial observations and conclusions were made a generation ago, but I still reckon the interview for the manager of the tourist office at La Bourboule went something like this:

Interviewer: 'I see you have all the qualifications and certification, so now for a couple of questions to test your aptitude and potential suitability.'

Interviewee: 'Of course.'

Interviewer: 'Very good. Do you like meeting people, especially foreigners?'

Interviewee: 'No and no, and especially foreigners.'

Interviewer: 'Good, good. And can you speak any foreign

languages?'

Interviewee (*hesitantly as if admitting to a guilty secret*): 'German, Dutch and Spanish fluently, and a little Japanese.'

Interviewer (*sadly*): 'Ah. I see. And what about English?'

Interviewee (*even more guiltily*): 'Yes.'

Interviewer (*hopefully*): 'But could you pretend to speak nothing but French when on desk duty and be really rude to any foreigners, especially the English?'

Interviewee (*brightening up*): 'Of course. It is in my nature.'

Interviewer (*happily*): 'Wonderful. The job is yours.'

We have been looking for a hotel, and think we have found one which will tick most of our boxes.

When it comes to finding somewhere to spend a night while on the road in France, our parameters are probably not the same as most people's. This is probably because we are mean and have never seen the sense in worrying about the wallpaper pattern or quality of furniture in a room in which you are going to lie unconscious for most of the time you are renting it.

In no particular order, our shopping list will include:

Price - the cheaper the better.

Location - hopefully away from a motorway or busy road but near lots of interesting bars and restaurants

Character/Ambience - the more unusual the better, as long as there are no full-time arsonists or axe murderers staying at the same time as us.

A late bar.

From the above you will see that our idea of a perfect lodging for a night is a cheap room above a characterful bar in a pedestrianised area of a town with lots of bars and entertainment places which shut before we want to go to bed and sleep.

We have struck lucky on many occasions, and I have particularly fond memories of a room in the then dodgy area of the port of Cherbourg. It was not until the morning we realised the significance of the red light outside the main entry. This also explains why the guests seemed to stay no longer than an hour, and the interesting propositions my wife got when sitting on her own at the bar.

But we have arrived at what looks to be a suitably old-fashioned and slightly run-down French hotel. By 'old-fashioned' in this context, I mean very informal, cheap, and with a proprietor caring more about the quality of the food served than whether anyone has bothered to service the rooms in the past month.

The Celtique is tucked away off the main road and approached through a yard wreathed by flags of all nations. From the outside it has that dilapidated air which shows the owners are not over concerned with appearances, and will thus not be too worried about house rules.

Inside we are met by a charming lady who delicately points out that payment should be in cash only. At 30 Euros a night and having caught the bouquet wafting from the kitchen, we take a room without bothering to look at it. I ask if we can have a drink on the terrace and Madame says she will send someone out to take our order. She does, and it is herself she has sent. After handing over and discussing the menu, she disappears to tell the chef what we will be eating. Later, we find she would have been talking to herself. The indefatigable woman also presided over the bar, made and served our breakfast and totted up our bill in the morning. We left her mounting the stairs with a bucket and mop.

We had dined very well in good company and the room had a bed, so we would certainly recommend the Celtique - or at least to visitors with inside leg measurements of over 30 inches. This is because, in our room at least, that was the eye-watering (for shorter-legged people) distance from the floor to the rim of the old-fashioned and otherwise charming sit-in bath. I am told by my wife that my inside leg measurement is a tad less than 30 inches, and there laid the rub.

*   *   *

It is time to move on from La Bourboule, but not before we take the waters. A visit to a bath house has never appeared on any things-to-do-before-I kick-the-bucket list, but it seems a shame not to see what all the fuss is about.

After loading the car and checking our underwear is fresh on (or at least my wife insists on checking mine), we join a procession of elderly people hobbling toward the Grand Spa of La Bourboule. It is a cinematic moment, and I realise I am reminded of the scene in *Soylent Green* where Edward G Robinson and assorted oldie extras are making a bee-line for the euthanasia centre.

Like the grand bath house at Le Mont-Dore, this one is an uneasy chimera of a 1970s bingo hall and a sultan's palace, and the lower floor is riven with huge picture windows bearing hugely blown-up photographs of the customers enjoying the facilities. Unlike the typical British gym, the photos do not show young and highly toned women. The gallery here shows eighty-year-olds waist-deep in the bubbling waters, and I comment how wrinkled their costumes are. My wife looks more closely, then points out that they are not in fact wearing costumes.

Inside, we find ourselves standing at a counter far below the glass bubble of a soaring cupola. Like the walls and floor, the counter is made of gleaming marble. Behind it is a woman dressed as if for a shift in the cosmetic department of a big store. After eyeing us up and down, she snaps a metaphorical finger to summon another even-more cosmetically-enhanced attendant. This leg of the relay takes us to an ante-room, where we are asked to sit at an interview desk. All around us, ladies of a certain age and far beyond are relaxing on loungers or having some form of primping treatment, and I begin to feel seriously out of place. For the next ten minutes we are quizzed about out dates of birth, political persuasion, star signs and collar

(48)

sizes in the usual French way. When we are asked what treatment we want, I ask for a menu. Looking at it, I see that the Grand Therme at La Bourboule is the European centre for treating respiratory infections and allergies. The price of treatment certainly takes my breath away, and the names leave me none the wiser.

Services on offer include individual or collective aerosol therapy, which sounds somehow threatening. Another option includes what are described as specific ORL treatments, ranging from tubular blowings to shower pharyngienne. There are also what they call drink cures, but I do not know if this means drinks which cure ailments, or cures which address a drinking problem. There is also something described as lashy dome, which sounds interesting but is priced at 100 Euros. After studying the options, my wife suggests we settle for a *Bain de Détente en Eau Calme*. As she says, it sounds relaxing and just happens to be the cheapest option on the menu.

Having heard the level of our ambitions and appearing to lose interest, our inquisitor presses a button in a somehow dismissive manner and two young women in businesslike white coats, skirts and pumps appear. One is a ravishingly beautiful blonde, with pouting, full lips and a more than passing resemblance to the young Brigitte Bardot. The other obviously spends a lot of time working out in the gym, and puts me in mind of Olympian javelinist Fatima Whitbread.

Unsurprisingly, my wife is led off to her treatment by the Sex Kitten, and I am invited to follow Fatima.

*   *   *

Ten minutes later, and I am laying in an old-fashioned and uncomfortable bath, half-filled with tepid water. I was left here by Fatima, whose only comment was to tell me to keep my bathers on for the sake of hygiene when I started to strip. Whilst waiting for something to happen, I work out that the cost of the treatment so far comes in at around two pounds a minute. I don't know what is to come, but it had better be good to justify the cost.

Another ten minutes pass, then the cubicle door opens. Fatima is wearing rubber gloves and apron, and I feel a frisson of nervous anticipation before she orders me out of the bath. Apparently, my treatment is over.

I am given a dressing gown and pair of disposable flip-flops and invited to join my wife in the relaxation area. Here, there is an unlimited supply of tisane (herbal tea), of which I drink copiously to try and get my money's worth. I also pocket the disposable flip-flops and try to smuggle the dressing gown off the premises, but am caught by Fatima.

*   *   *

Feeling fleeced rather than re-invigorated, we are walking to the car when I see in a hairdresser's shop window that La Bourboule offers other even more unusual services than the Grande Therme. Written in English by someone to whom it is not a familiar language, one poster advertises courses in Turkish belly dangling, while another offers dog wanking.

This thought-provoking service is overshadowed by one of the list of treatments and services offered by the establishment. Impressively sign-written in French, they include hair styling and cutting, highlighting and dyeing and, I swear, fanny feeling.

Avèze

I suppose because of the impervious granite obstacles it meets when searching for the easiest route to the sea, the Dordogne does seem to meander like a hornet drunk on fermented fruit. If it ran from source to estuary as straight as a crow is alleged to fly, its length would be halved. But then there would be fewer fascinating places to visit en route.

We have been following the Dordogne's erratic progress in a roughly north-westerly direction, through Saint-Sauves-d'Auvergne and Messeix, heading for the famed gorges of Avèze. The landscape has changed dramatically, as the towering mountains of the Massif Central lay behind and out of sight, and for the moment we could be in Normandy or even Hampshire.

Narrow, winding lanes pass by tree and hedge-lined fields and lead us through a succession of sleepy villages. Some appear more comatose then sleepy, but each has its church, school and shop with post office agency. This indicates someone must live here, though we have not seen a sign of life for many a mile. The lack of humanity cannot be because it is the time of the sacred midday meal, and as we have heard of no deadly plague falling suddenly on this part of the country and the Tour de France does not start till the end of the month, this must be a particularly unpopulated part of France*. We are, to be fair, more than a little off the tourist trail.

Arriving eventually at Avèze, we pull up by the church. We have yet to spot a human being, but there are other signs of life. In a barnyard across the road at least a hundred hens are contentedly going about their business. They are being kept in order by a handful of strutting males, and you can see where the expression cocksure has its origins. Some would say that the strutting cock is also a very appropriate national symbol when you think of a certain type of French male.

Geese and ducks and goats and the odd pig also

wander amiably around the yard and it is a delight to see such peaceful co-habitation. Then I detect a human presence.

Sitting on a three-legged kitchen chair which is using a wall of the dilapidated barn for support is a very old man. Beside him is a dog which must be as old as he in relative terms. Both are soaking up the sun, and it seems to me that there is something wistful about the way the man is looking at the strutting cockerels. He is perhaps thinking of the faraway days of his own youth and *puissance*, and I am reminded that we are the only species which is aware of our mortality. The old spaniel shifts and grunts in discomfort, and the man lays a soothing hand on its head. It is probably puzzled and irritated by the pains of old age, but at least it does not know what is to come.

The man sees we are watching him and nods a greeting. I lift our flask of coffee in silent invitation. He reaches down and produces a bottle containing a straw-coloured liquid from beside his chair and beckons us over. I mentally rub my hands in anticipation as we climb the low wall. Encounters like this are why we so love being off the beaten track in France *profonde*.

*Looking up the stats later, I found that the Auvergne is one of the least-populated regions in Europe. At 1.3 million people occupying an area of 10,000 square miles, this gives a population density of 52 people for every square kilometre. As the population density of our home town of Portsmouth is 5000 per sq. kilometre, you can see why we have grown to love the less occupied part of France.

*   *   *

After what we have seen elsewhere, we find the Gorges of Avèze a bit of a disappointment. Our idea of a proper gorge can be found in the Ardeche or most spectacularly at Verdon.

Whilst not contravening the Trades Description Act as to

what qualifies as a gorge, these seem more like deep and steep tree-lined valleys.

The corkscrew road eventually leads us down to a bridge which seems an ideal place to set up a picnic. My wife unpacks the portable stove and packets of bacon and eggs, and I wander along the river bank to chat to a couple of fishermen. They are both in the international uniform of serious anglers, and it has always puzzled me that they feel the need to dress like soldiers trying to blend in with their surroundings. Perhaps they believe it will hide them from their prey, or deter passers-by like me who insist on talking to them.

As well as the usual camouflage clothing, the men have more fishing rods deployed than they have fingers. In France we have noted that fishing seems more about results than sport or relaxation. In England, a man will sit on a beach all night returning home with an empty bag but full of contentment. Here, it is all about numbers. I once fished at a trout lake in Normandy where a man regularly walked around the shore dumping dustbin loads of fish into the water at the very feet of the anglers.

I ask the men how their day is going, and am thoughtless enough to say we have not been impressed by the local gorges. Looking as if I have questioned the honour of his mother, the larger one asks where we have come from before observing that we have clearly not bothered to get out of our car. The river is inaccessible to vehicles for fifteen miles from La Bourboule to this spot, and runs through what is more than probably the finest gorge in all France. He and his friend have walked it while fishing many times, but he knows that English tourists like to stay in their cars and miss the sights which are really worth seeing.

I consider taking on his implied challenge and getting my hiking boots on, then remember that the only books I have read about this stretch of the river were by people who did not walk it. It must therefore be pretty inaccessible to even the fittest and enthusiastic of explorers.

The fishermen have obviously taken umbrage, things are

getting a bit heated, and I am reminded of the scene in *Deliverance* where one of the townies falls foul of a group of sex-starved hillbillies.

Even though I cannot see myself running that risk, I back down, apologise for insulting their gorges, then maliciously ask if they fancy a bacon and egg sandwich made with the best English white sliced bread. The couple do not actually make the sign of the cross, but horror suffuses their ruddy faces as they contemplate the proposal.

I shrug and tell them they do not know what they are missing, but their faces and manner suggest they do, and are very glad of it.

*   *   *

We are completely lost, but unconcerned as this is a common occurrence. I put it down to my wife's inability to read a map properly; she puts it down to all our maps being either a decade out of date or part of cheap atlases which devote one small page to a whole region of France.

Theoretically, of course, all we need to do is follow the river. This is what people do in books and films when cutting their way through dense jungle. It is not so easy when you are in a car and have literally run out of road. This is a first for us, as the road we have followed under the directions of the unfriendly fishermen terminates in a totally isolated dwelling-place. We have found ourselves at the bottom of many a dead-end lane, but this is our first dead-end village.

As the inevitable row looms about whose fault it is, succour appears in the shape of a bright yellow van which comes to a wheel-skidding, dust-enveloping stop alongside. It is La Poste to the rescue.

I have encountered hundreds of postmen and women in my time in France, and most have been jolly, helpful and completely mad when behind the wheel. But, the driving behaviour and standards of the typical French *facteur* is another French stereotype which is absolutely spot-on. In my years in France I have been rammed three times by kamikaze postman. The most recent incident was when we drew up behind a parked van to ask for directions. Before we could get out of the car, the *Monsieur le facteur* walked quickly from the gate, jumped in and roared backwards, staving in the front of our car. Rather than apologising for not looking where he was going, he said that we should not have been in his way, so it was all our fault. We were surprised and pleased that La Poste agreed to pay for all repairs to our car without the slightest quibble. Then a postman friend explained that their drivers cause so many accidents a year that it is cheaper for the company just to pay up and not make a fight of it.

Bort-les-Orgues

Again we find ourselves unimpressed with a natural feature which the guide books and locals make a fuss about.

Bort-les-Orgues lies at the foot of an old volcano, boasts an impressive medieval château, and is the birthplace of the renowned philosopher Marmontel. He is one of those thinkers thought enough of to be known by one name and I am a fan, though generally do not think much of French philosophers who made their names in the Age of Reason. Most seemed to have immensely rich parents and spent their days looking down from their castles on the peasants toiling in the fields and coming up with observations about humanity which were mostly statements from the Department of the Bleedin' Obvious.

Marmontel was an exception, as he was from a very poor family and worked his way up the social ladder with a mix of hard work and cunning. Anyone who could win the patronage of Madame de Pompadour must have been a force to be reckoned with. John Ruskin included Marmotel in a very short list of the three people who had had the most influence on his life, which is good enough for me.

Despite this and other reasons to be proud, the town is named for an outcrop of rock, overlooking the river and said to look like a set of organ pipes.

The lumps of basalt we are studying look to me nothing like organ pipes, and I am only half-joking when I propose visiting the local *Marie* to complain that we have been short changed. As we return to the car I make a sarcastic comment to an old man sitting on a bench and enjoying the view of the river far below. He gives the standard reaction of a look mixed with bemusement and horror at my brutal treatment of his language, then points out that the outcrop across the river is not the famed organ pipes. When I tell him we were led here by a representative of La Poste, he gives a Gallic shrug and asks why he should be surprised that a postman has made a delivery to the wrong address.

A little later and we are admiring the orgues of Bort, which - with a good degree of suspension of disbelief - could be taken for a row of petrified organ pipes. We came up a winding track to the viewpoint, and found the closest the French come to a tea stall under the shelter of some trees. Tea was not on the menu at the cabin, but we bought an ice cream and looked out over the river.

After the ankle-deep disappointment of La Bourboule, the Dordogne is now a proper river, flowing deep, wide and handsome. Over the next seventy five miles it will drop nearly a thousand feet, which explains the size and significance of the four great dams built to harness the wild energy of the water. The first is the Barrage de Bort, on which work began in 1942. It took three years and cost the lives of 25 men to finish it, and engineering setbacks included an avalanche.

The other main attraction here is the Château du Val. It is sturdily attractive in a medieval way, with distinctive pepper pot roofs. There are guided tours of the inside, but the man at the snack bar tells us it is not worth the money. He tells us the château was bought by France's national electricity supplier (EDF) in 1946, and gifted to the town. The commune had spent a fortune on restoring and improving the exterior but neglected the inside, so there is nothing much to see. He says it is all show with nothing behind the windows, and I try and explain our equivalent expression about all fur coat and no knickers. It does not translate well in French, but we take his advice, abandon the idea of the tour and settle for another rum and raisin ice cream apiece.

*   *   *

We have spent the afternoon moving slowly along the river, stopping off at the viewpoint at St Nazaire and exploring the terrain inland.

We are in the department of the Corrèze, which was once and may still be the poorest place in France. The soil is thin and poor, and, in parts of the region, the moorland and peat bogs are reminiscent of Cornwall and Brittany. There is also lots of water and wildlife. Wolves were declared extinct here at the turn of the 20th century but the department abounds with other creatures of the wild.

This part of France has much to recommend it if you like rugged beauty and a feel of the rural past. Viewed from our snug comfort zones, it seems it would have been an idyllic time and place in which to live the simple life. Those who lived in grinding if picturesque poverty probably had a different view.

Mauriac

We have reached a significant point in our journey. By following the meanderings of the river we have left the Limousin and are back in the Auvergne. This is the department of Cantal and the changes in landscape, customs and cultures are also marked by the number of towns and villages with names that end with 'ac'.

Mauriac is a little way from the river, but worth the diversion. It is a town of some repute, known for its horse fair, former Benedictine Abbey, past marble quarrying activities, its special breed of beef cattle and Cantal cheese. This is one of our favourite of the 300-odd official varieties found in France. Although it would please neither the French nor English producers to hear me say so, we find the mature version almost identical to Cheddar.

Perhaps most importantly from a cultural perspective, Mauriac is said to be the last bastion of the Occitan language. Or, if you prefer, the *langue d'oc*, which is where the former province got its name.

It is an ancient language which had a surprising spread, and was and is spoken still in parts of Italy, Monaco and Spain. It is still in fact the official language of the Catalan region. The original users sound an agreeable race, as 'oc' in their language means 'yes'.

We will do some digging around in the ancient market town in the morning, but as the day grows long we need to find a satisfactory lodging for the night. Thus my first job is to look round for a suitable bar. This is because the right sort of bar will be a much better centre of information than the most efficient tourist office. And providing I stand a few drinks, we are likely to get a much friendlier reception.

As specially trained dogs are good at finding drugs in airport luggage, even my wife admits I have something of a nose for sniffing out this sort of bar.

I worked out recently that we must have visited around 4000 bars in France over thirty years of wandering. The largeness of the number is not just because I like a drink, but because we stop at a bar for coffee and perhaps directions and local colour at least twice a day when on the road and in an unfamiliar region.

Most people's idea of a typical French bar is based upon something they have seen in a film, a visit to a big town or what British owners and operators think their customers think what a French bar should be like. I do not recognise these exotic and generally unfriendly places with waiters in long white aprons, eye-wateringly expensive food served on square plates and wine at a cost per glass that would buy a bottle or two in a proper French bar. It is also a fact that proper French bars do not travel abroad, just as Ye Olde Red Lion in France or Spain will usually be nothing like a proper English pub.

Of course, there are various categories within the genre. Like English pubs, a French bar may appear in several guises. For those not familiar with the general classification, one with rooms and food in the countryside will be called an *auberge*. A *bistro* is a bar selling reasonably priced food. For some reason I have not figured out, some bistros insist on calling themselves bistrots. The classic rural French bar will either sell no food, or do a lunchtime special. Some will be favoured by truck drivers and are included in posh guides. Others will serve an *ouvrier* (workman's) meal at midday and most likely close when the last diner leaves.

We are looking for a bang-on drinking-only bar, and I think we have located one in a back street not too far from the town centre. It is open and called the *Rendezvous des Pêcheurs*, which is a good start. Names can tell you a lot about a French bar, and so can what is going on outside. Above the door of this one is not a neon representation, but a genuine classic red 'cigar' in the shape of two cones joined at the base which used to mark out bars which also sell tobacco.

The plate glass window has been filmed with the smoke from a million cigarettes, and is dressed with a lace curtain which has seen better days. The light of day is also being kept out by dozens of faded posters. Having taken the trouble to put them up, many bar owners like to get full use of those they agree to display. One in this window is for a village fete, and the date and ticket price show it took place before the change from Franc to Euro.

Even better, leaning against the window is what looks like an original *Mobylette*. Once upon a time, millions of French working men would own one of these sturdy mopeds, and every village would have a shop and mechanic who could fix it along with bicycles, tractors and Citroën *Deau Chevaux*. As times got better, more and more countrymen could afford cars and the Mobylette factory closed. The irony is that nowadays an original Mobylette can fetch a better price than a brand new scooter.

All in all and together with other indicators, the Rendezvous des Pêcheurs looks like our sort of bar.

*   *   *

On a technical note, there are 2500 varieties of flowers found in the Auvergne, and a hundred plants which are protected. One of them is used to make possibly the foulest drink in all France...and perhaps all Europe.

Previously I had thought the runaway winner of that title would be Suze, which is also made from the gentian flower. On the basis that the worst a medicine tastes the most effective it must be, Suze is claimed by fans to be a restorative for the liver and a sure-fire hangover cure. Thanks to my new friends at the Rendezvous des Pêcheurs, I now know there is an even more evil concoction.

According to the landlord and his cronies, *Salers* the drink shares its name with a beef cattle and a cheese. It looks and tastes as if it has been made with cattle dung. All areas have their favoured home brew, and had I asked for a glass of the local liquor in Normandy, I would have been set up with a glass of apple brandy. In the Angevin area of the Loire Valley it would have been a classy rosé or a fearsome eau-de-vie distilled from baby plums. Here I was assured by

Freddo and his fishing friends at the RDP that Salers is to this area as nectar was to the gods.

When I took a sniff and thought I had been given a dose of the patron's cough medicine, I should have politely declined. But never one to risk damaging the sometimes fragile status of entente cordiale existing between our two nations, I held my breath and drank it straight down. This was a mistake, as my glass was immediately refuelled. It was not until the bottle was emptied that I noticed that, loud as my drinking companions were in its praise, I was the only one drinking it.

*   *   *

Several hours later and I am mid-way through a fine steak which tastes nothing remotely like but bears the same name as the devil's brew I was recently subjected. There is to be a wodge of Salers cheese afterwards, and the promise of more fine conversation with the party on the next table.

Freddo the patron of the RDP having directed us to a hidden treasure of a restaurant, we found ourselves seated beside a Parisian who taught French in Manchester schools for many years. Thankfully, none of the Mancunian accent has rubbed off on his impeccable English, and we became soul mates when I declared my love of Maupassant's *Bel Ami*.

We end the evening sitting on the terrace under a huge moon, discussing the finer points of Dada-ism, though I am absolutely ignorant of what it is or was. This demonstrates the power of drink to open the mind and expand the consciousness, or at least make you believe that this is happening.

Food and Drink

Perhaps surprisingly, a quarter of the country's hundreds of official cheeses are produced in the Auvergne. Cantal is one of the country's oldest, and is mentioned by Roman historian Pliny the Elder two thousand years ago.

Similar in texture and appearance if not taste, Salers owes its distinctive flavour to the pastureland around the town for which it is named. It takes 400 litres of milk from Salers cows to make a single 40k wheel.

As mentioned previously, Saint-Nectaire is highly prized for its hazelnutty flavour. Also as mentioned earlier, Murol is a close relation.

One of the best-known and best-loved regional cheeses is Bleu D'Auvergne, which strikes non-aficionados like me as tasting like a saltier (and far more expensive) equivalent of Danish Blue. Bleu de Laqueuille is the original version, and said to have been invented by a farmer with a needle and some mouldy bread who was trying to create a Roquefort-type cheese.

Back in the 9th century, Fourme D'Ambert was used as a currency to pay pasture rent.

Other notable cheeses from the region include Savaron, Montagne, Gaperon and Cabécou. Tomme d'Auvergne is a flavoursome cheese used in a traditional potato dish (see below). There are, of course, hundreds more excellent varieties made informally on farms and in monasteries and homes across the region. I have done my best to sample all the official and unofficial French cheeses we come across, and have the blood pressure and cholesterol readings to prove it.

In general terms, any region's culinary traditions will reflect its location and what flourishes there. The Auvergne is many a mile from the sea and even the locals would admit that a place full of volcanoes and granite sub-strata is going to mean that soil can be a bit thin on the ground. An interesting reflection on the soil situation is the number of picturesque *pigeonniers* still to be seen across the region. The inmates were not kept as much for food as for their droppings. Pigeon guano was used to dress the fields, and was so strong in nitrates that it could not be put on land until it was raining lest it burn the crops. Until the Revolution, the local liege lord had the monopoly on pigeon poo. Nowadays there are more sophisticated forms of fertilizer, but *pigeonniers* are terribly trendy as must-have embellishments to one's second home.

The cuisine of the Auvergne would probably be described as 'hearty' in a guidebook, which is PR speak for generally heavy and simple dishes.

It is said that the mountain air is particularly good for drying salted meat, which is either an excuse or good reason for the amount of sausage and other cooked meats produced in the region. Varieties may be enhanced with hazelnuts, bilberries, or chestnut. Cured raw ham is another speciality of the Auvergne, and is still produced in villages and even individual inns.

The production of candied fruit and fruit pastes and 'dry' jams has a long tradition in the region. The fearsome Cardinal Richelieu had a soft spot for candied apricots, and vast fields of angelica were once an everyday sight around Cleremont-Ferrand

(the stems were candied). Other sweet-toothed specialties include chocolate-coated almonds and blackberry caramels.

The Auvergne is another area known for its chestnuts, which in the form or flour become a whole variety of breads and cakes. There's also a chestnut liqueur. At the top end of the gastro-indicator are truffles, and in autumn and winter they can be found in most markets. There will often be photographic evidence on the stall, showing the hunter and his dog in action.

Soupe de lentilles aux tomates

When you think about it, only the French could make such a fuss about a humble pulse. After all, what other country would form a solemn and exclusive association to honour the rice pudding?

The tiny *lentille de Puy* conforms perfectly to the requirements of food snobbery, where something originally regarded as peasant fodder becomes an icon of a region's gastronomic culture and creativity. Naturally, this means that those who produce or serve the item can charge a fortune for doing so.

The Auvergne produces 60 percent of all lentils grown in France, and there is of course an *appellation de origine controlée* (*see below*) ensuring that only lentils grown in or near Le Puy-en-Velay and sticking to the rules of the AOC can call themselves Puy lentils.

Although it sounds a bit contradictory, the producers say that it is the rich volcanic soil of the Auvergne coupled with the difficult growing conditions which give the little green gems the distinctive flavour and high nutritional value. Interestingly, they are grown without water or fertilizer.

Despite their exotic and privileged provenance (and comparative price), Puy lentils cook the same way as their humbler relatives. You simply rinse them in cold water and add to a pot containing around six times the volume of water, then bring to the boil and simmer for twenty minutes. This is a simple but classic regional recipe using Puy lentils:

Ingredients

Two peeled and chopped onions

Four sliced carrots

Two stalks of celery, chopped

Two cloves of pressed or finely chopped garlic

A quarter of a cup of olive oil

Six cups of vegetable stock

500 grams of uncooked Puy lentils

A can of pulped tomatoes

A bouquet garni

Two tablespoons of wine vinegar

Some seasoning

Method

Heat the olive oil in a heavy pot, then add the onions, carrots, celery and garlic.

Cook on a medium heat, stirring occasionally for ten minutes or until the vegetables start to brown.

Add the stock, then the lentils, canned tomatoes and bouquet garni.

Bring to the boil, then simmer heartily.

Cover partly with a lid and cook for at least half an hour or until the lentils are tender.

Towards the end of cooking, stir in the wine vinegar and season to taste.

Truffade

Pork is the meat most likely to be found on an Auvergne table, often stuffed inside cabbage leaves, and often served with *truffade*. This is a cheesy potato dish which, for us, examples the very best of cooking Auvergne-style. Here's how it's done:

Ingredients

One kilogram of firm-fleshed potatoes

150g smoked bacon bits or lardons as the French call them

Two garlic cloves

400g Tomme d'Auvergne cheese (or as near as you can get)

Method

Cook the bacon/lardons gently in a heavy pan, adding the garlic when the fat is flowing.

Peel the potatoes, cut into thin-ish slices and add to the pan.

Cook for fifteen minutes or so or until the potatoes are done, then add the cheese.

Mess around with the dish until the cheese has melted in and you have a deliciously gooey sort of potato-cheese cake.

Serve with a little chopped parsley.

Pounti du Cantal aux Pruneaux

This is a really interesting specialty of the region and department. *Pounti* is found in various guises all across the Auvergne, and is basically a meat loaf. It might be made from a variety of meats or even vegetarian; this one uses prunes:

Ingredients

500g sausage meat

25g prunes

75g flour

250ml milk

Two eggs

A small onion

50g shallots

50g parsley

250g chard

A packet of baking powder

Method

Chop the onions, shallots, parsley and chard.

Mix with the sausage meat.

Combine the flour, eggs, milk and then the baking powder and add to the sausage meat mixture.

Put the mixture into a suitable cake or bread tin, alternating a layer of prunes and a layer of mixture.

Bake in a moderate oven for half an hour or until the mix is firm and ready.

Apple Flognarde

This Auvergne and Limousin favourite is similar to the perhaps better-known *clafoutis*, and is essentially a baked 'soufflé' with fruit. You can use virtually any soft fruit, but apple is a favourite in this neck of the French woods:

Ingredients

Three eating apples

Two cups full fat milk

Three large eggs

Half cup flour

Half cup sugar

Two tablespoons of vegetable oil

One teaspoon vanilla extract

Zest of lemon

Method

Pre-heat oven to 225°C.

Core, peel and slice the apples.

Arrange the apples artistically in a suitable pie dish (about 8 inches).

Whisk the flour, milk, eggs, sugar, oil, vanilla extract and zest and pour over the apples.

Bake for the best part of an hour, or until the apples are browned and the batter puffed up.

Don't panic when the 'soufflé' deflates.

Serve with cream or ice cream.

Drink

The Auvergne is one of the oldest wine growing areas in France, but its wines are little known outside the region. In fact it was not until 2009 that the region began to produce any Appellation Contrôlée (AOC)* wines. The climate produces light, fresh and fruity wines, dominated by reds from the Gamay grape. Paradoxically for a region not known for its wines, it is hard to find an allotment, patch of spare ground or even a roundabout without a few vines being kept on them. The region specialises in *Vin de Paille*, named for its method of production.

Instead of the wine-making process beginning immediately after the harvest, the grapes are left on straw to dry out. Though picked in September and October, it can be as late as the following February before the grapes are dry enough for the producer. By then the sugar content has rocketed, and the fermentation process can take another six months. Some straw wines can be matured in barrels for up to two years. This leads to a heady alcoholic content of up to twenty degrees.

An Appellation de Origine Contrôlée is best described as a physical and intellectual copyright, or a licence granted by the government to officially control quality of product.

LEG 2

Mauriac to Beaulieu-sur-Dordogne

Distance: 85 kilometres

Regions: The Auvergne, Limousin

Departments: Cantal, Corrèze

We awake, much refreshed and in comparatively luxurious surroundings.

The rain is relentless, so last evening we splashed out for a posh log cabin at Mauriac's municipal campsite. The site comes highly recommended and is living up to its reputation. Although we have stayed at some decidedly dodgy places, it is surprising how often campsites run by the commune are better-appointed and cheaper than commercial ones.

The day has begun with mild disappointment when we learn that the old train service through Mauriac which took passengers on a sometimes spectacular route through valleys and gorges and over soaring viaducts is no longer in existence.

It would have been a most sentimental of journeys, as I first rode on a narrow-gauge railway through this region when I hitch-hiked around Europe in the mid-Sixties. In recall, it seems more than half a lifetime ago, and was a completely unforgettable experience. Things were changing rapidly then, but some parts of the most rural areas were closer in spirit and sometimes substance to the previous century. It sounds a tall traveller's tale, but I cherish the crystal-clear memory of watching an elderly and wizened little man in a beret as we chugged through the hinterland. He was ploughing a field, but-quite seriously- with an ox rather than a tractor. He did not respond to my wave, but stood watching almost wistfully as we puffed away up the slope. Then he spat on his hands and returned to a back-breaking travail which would have been familiar to his ancestors.

The railway was axed by a Gallic equivalent of Dr Beeching in 1994. Nowadays I suppose people use their cars on a far quicker but much less interesting journey westwards. It's a fair bet there are no oxen ploughing the thin soil hereabouts, unless it is in a display of traditional country pursuits.

Salers

Another detour from the river's course, this time to check out one of the at least fifty ancient villages claiming to be the most beautiful/unspoiled/best restored/unrestored in all France.

Although it is not the high season, we have joined a huge scrimmage of visitors fighting their way into Salers. The town which gave its name to (or took its name from) a breed of cattle, a cheese and a foul drink must also be one of the most expensive places to park. Most unusually, it is patrolled, and by tough-looking men with outfits apparently modelled on those of the scary national riot police, the CRS.

As well as one of the most beautiful villages, Salers is allegedly one of the highest; at 300 metres I reckon the views from the ramparts are certainly worth crowing about.

Even if some of its claims are overblown, Salers does contain some fine examples of ancient buildings from the Middle Ages to the Renaissance. Once it boasted a fine castle, but it was razed to the ground in the 17th century on the orders of the king. This was because the town had become a Protestant stronghold. So, across the years Salers has become used to being under siege. Given the cost of parking and general price levels, perhaps the descendants of the original inhabitants are getting their own back.

Many of the rugged buildings are made of lava stone, and 'fish-scale' * tiled roofs are common. France does these sort of restored or allegedly untouched-by-time towns and villages very well, but it is a sad truth that the sort of overpriced, vulgar tat on offer to visitors is the same from Mont St Michel to Carcassonne.

We are swept along by the crowd, keeping our eyes to the front in case a shopkeeper charges us for looking into his window. I notice that some of the goods on show are literally priceless. This is possibly because the owners are ashamed of such naked avarice. Or perhaps they know that showing the asking prices will stop potential customers coming through the doors. It is even possible that those traders who boldly feature their prices are hoping the level will cause heart attacks amongst the tide of humanity, causing a stoppage right outside their shop.

Apart from the price of everything, the most notable and noticeable aspect of our visit is that everyone is taking photographs. This was always the case in touristic venues, but the advent of digital and phone cameras has made capturing every single item or activity an obsession.

All around us, people are taking photographs of every building they pass, regardless of its appeal or historical significance. Those with zoom capability are snapping individual windows and doors and other features. I even see one man focussing on a dog turd outside the entrance to a bar. Others are marshalling members of their family for group shots, and some people are photographing people photographing other people. Sandwiched amongst the original buildings is a plate glass and aluminium-fronted convenience store, but the frenzy does not abate and I see people actually taking snaps of a window display of tinned goods.

Our feet are hardly touching the ground as the pressure from behind impels us forward, and when we see a bar looming up we throw ourselves from the throng like parachutists bailing out on D-Day.

I wait as a passer-by photographs the menu, then pick it up to see what is on offer. There is a branch of Credit Agricole occupying an ancient building opposite, and I consider nipping over to apply for a loan so we can eat. In the end we settle for one coffee between us, and I ask for a glass of tap water from the clearly contemptuous waiter.

After paying for the coffee and pointedly leaving the waiter untipped we dive back into the melee, ensuring we do not try to go against the tide. At the nearest exit point we repeat the parachute process, and make our way down a steep slope to the car park. A stony-faced attendant is hovering near our car, and when I ask him to smile so I can take a photograph of him, his scowl deepens. When I ask him to say 'Salers' and explain about the English tradition of the photographer asking the subject to say 'cheese', he either does not get it or is holding out for a fee.

*As proved so effective with ancient armour, overlapping roof tiles in the style and shape of fish scales are a particularly attractive feature on many old buildings in this part of France.

Chavignac, Auriac, Servières-le-Château

We are back alongside the river and passing through the little village of Chavignac. From now on we will be able to follow the undulations of the river for some miles as it heads south-west for Argentat.

Leaving the village we see a sign for Auriac, and decide to take a look at the capital of the Cantal department, which is also the umbrella capital of France. It is a fascinating if little publicised fact that more than half the brollies produced in the country are made in Auriac. For some possibly related reason, the town has a totally unjustified reputation as the coldest place in this part of France.

On the way we see a bi-lingual notice advertising a Middle-Aged Farm and pull over to take a look at least from the outside. I am fascinated by the idea of seeing herds of people of advancing years grazing contentedly in fields or discussing their medical conditions over feeding troughs. Then I realise the attraction is that the farm is run using medieval methods and equipment. From what we have seen over the years this does not make it a lot different from many farms in deepest France, but at this one there is the added incentive. For a small additional fee, visitors are invited to try their hand at using a scythe. This shows real enterprise, as presumably it will be the first time that a farmer will be paid by the people harvesting his crops rather than the other way round. I note there is a privately-operated ambulance sitting in a lay-by near the gate, so perhaps the lessons are in full swing. And the driver is hoping to pick up a bit of accidental business.

A couple of miles along the sign-laden road there is a large placard exhorting passers-by not to miss the Towers of Merle.

The sign does not say how far away the towers are, but we take the turning indicated and follow the logical rule of keeping going on the same road until instructed otherwise. This, as we have often found, is not always the way things are done in France.

After several miles of tower-less horizons, we stop and ask directions from a woman who is beating a cow in a field. She leaves off long enough to tell us our destination is indeed *tout droit* (straight on), but what she calls a good journey. I ask her why she is beating the cow and she says it is easier than beating her husband. The cow does not feel it and she can pretend it is him.

Eventually we hit a sign for the Towers of Merle, which promises all will be revealed only a kilometre distant. As usual, we find this claim would only be true if we were driving a Formula One car or a Harrier jump jet. It is an incontrovertible rule that roadside signs in France always underestimate the distance to an attraction, particularly if it is a supermarket. Perhaps measurements are different in rural areas, and it is from France that the English expression about 'a country mile' comes from.

We check our emergency rations and spare petrol cans and press on. No more than half an hour later, we spot some gaunt ruins in a valley apparently riven with water courses. From this distance and with a bit of imagination, one can imagine how foreboding the twin towers would have looked in their pomp.

According to our guide book, the *Tours de Merle* are what remains of a fortified site dating back to the 12th century. By the 16th century, Merle had acquired all of seven castles and a village living off them. The original stronghold was built on a huge rocky outcrop surrounded on three sides by an ox-bow in the Maronne river, which was and still is a tributary of the Dordogne.

Merle reached the zenith of its importance after the marriage of Henry Plantagenet and Eleanor of Aquitaine in 1151, when the stronghold became a frontier post between the English-owned Duchy and the rest of France. The rocks beneath the ruins are riddled with caves in which dwelled a tribe of eccentrics known in the local dialect as *cafolene*, or mad dogs.

Hoping we might find some of them at home, we boot up and take the steep and sometimes dangerous track down into the valley and across the river. At the gates, we find our way blocked. Not by mad troglodytes or men-at-arms, though. Although it is the open season, it is also lunchtime so naturally the fortress is shut to visitors.

*   *   *

We have stopped for lunch at a roadside bar, and I am pleased to chalk up another addition to my collection of Unusual and Interesting Conveniences.

I began this harmless hobby many years ago with the intention of perhaps one day publishing a guide. It would be like a *relais routier* or hotel guide, only aimed at those interested in truly remarkable conveniences. It has become a harmless and occasionally rewarding pastime, and some have been remarkable for their condition, design, plumbing or other features. Over the years we have come across toilets a good distance from the bar, or sometimes in a neighbouring house. Once we followed the directions of the patron and went through the open door of the cottage next door, which we believed to be his. We found the bathroom and did our business, then smiled and nodded on our way out at the family seated at lunch in the front room. As we left, my wife observed how they had been arranged around the table in a frozen tableau with forks half way to open mouths. In the bar, we found that we had turned left instead of right and used someone else's facilities.

As to unusual designs in the Inventive Facilities category, I once used a urinal composed of a large metal funnel hanging from a piece of string in the back yard of an isolated bar. It was connected to a length of hosepipe, and out of curiosity I traced its length. I found the end laying alongside a row of dwarf peas in the vegetable garden. The French are very fond of puns and other word-play jokes, and I made one to the landlord based on 'peas' and 'pees', but it did not work in French.

Today's entry is a unisex affair through a curtain at the end of a passageway, and is an original *toilette turque*. This is a stand-and-deliver affair which is basically a hole in the ground. More sophisticated varieties have a ceramic tray and even the raised outline of a pair of feet to advise on the most effective and safest place to stand. Once upon a time they were commonplace throughout France, and, like zinc bars, are making a comeback in some trendy venues. Although the French refer to them as Turkish, a Turk will tell you the credit should be given to the Greeks. It can be argued that they are more hygienic than a standard sit-on bowl as there is no point of contact, but the standing/squatting position can mean the gruesome evidence of a lack of accuracy greeting the next user.

This one was distinguished by having a particularly savage flushing system, activated by pushing a button on exit. I pressed it before fully leaving the cubicle, and soaked the front of my trousers from the waist down. I tried to disguise the evidence by walking out of the bar with an unfolded road map held in a strategic position, but am sure I heard a guffaw of laughter as we reached the car. It was obviously an amusing diversion for the locals, and perhaps explained the chalked tally on a blackboard by the passageway leading to the lavatory.

*   *   *

Having stopped off to inspect the 65-hectare Lac Feyt and found it no more or less exciting than other lakes, we pause to wonder at the giant Barrage du Chastang. This huge hydro-electric dam is 85 metres high and has a volume of more than a quarter of a million cubic metres of concrete, based on granite. It is unlike most other dams as it has the remains of a 12th-century Abbey literally embedded in the dam.

Suitably impressed, we press on to the village of Servières-le-Château. The castle from which it gets its name is quite impressive, but on arrival we thought we had stumbled on a remake of the sci-fi 1950's classic film, *The day the Earth Stood Still*. Enquiry revealed that the metal disk-shaped monstrosity alongside the château was not meant to be a flying saucer, but an avant-garde exhibition centre. Sometimes I really do find it puzzling how a nation which is said to lead the world in fashion and design can come up with such totally unsuitable eyesores in the name of modernity.

Argentat

As we head for the start of Dordogneshire, the riverside road is littered with truly impressive dwelling places. Not grand *châteaux*, but big, solid houses surrounded by open terrain and just a stroll from the river. The thing about these large and imposing properties is that one rarely sees any sign of life in or around them. We have concluded that the owners are either elderly people who do not get out and about much, or holiday homes for those rich enough not to bother to visit them often.

If we were unimpressed by some of the villages and towns visited earlier today, Argentat more than makes up for earlier disappointment.

At this stage of its journey, the Dordogne is in full majesty. Road and river traffic to and from Bordeaux, Bergerac and other important wine-producing centres made it a place of some significance from early times. Before the railway put paid to the river as a principle means of transport, this was a thriving river port famed for the skills of its boatmen.

We drive down to the cobbled quay below the bridge and admire the old houses lining the bank. The first floor was for living and the ground floor for the animals, which probably paid dividends for the owners when the river flooded. Most have rustic type wooden balconies overlooking the Dordogne, and the steeply-pitched roofs are tiled with roughly hewn slabs of a brown local stone known as *Lauzes*. The combined weight of the tiles must be enormous, but the stout chestnut frames have been bearing their load with ease for centuries and show no signs of flagging.

We take coffee on the quay, and it is easy to imagine the scene here a couple of hundred years earlier.

The quayside would be piled high with goods being loaded on to a line of *gabares*. These huge, flat-bottomed barges were built on the river to a length of twenty metres with a beam of four. In contrast, the freeboard (distance between the water and deck) was a modest one metre. The Dordogne was shallow in parts even before the modern dams were set in place, and despite having hardly anything below the waterline the heavily laden craft could only make the perilous journey during one month in the springtime.

Up to three hundred of the slow-moving barges would make the six day journey. Ironically, those which survived would never return to their home port, being broken up for lumber and firewood at journey's end.

The fleets would be carrying local cheeses and fruit and honey and coal from nearby mines. There would be tons of chestnut poles harvested from the great forests of the Corrèze and destined for Bordeaux for use in the vineyards. Some would be carrying the finest oak staves to make wine casks for the cellars of grand *châteaux*. To make full use of the waterway at other times, flat-bottomed sailing scows (*courpet*) plied their trade to all parts within reach of the river.

Argentat prospered and grew steadily through the 18th and 19th centuries, then came a double whammy. An outbreak of deadly *phylloxera** devastated the region's vineyards, then in 1904, the railways arrived to deliver the *coup-de-grâs* to the river trade. There are still *gabares* to be found on the water at Argentat, but their only cargo will be tourists on a pleasure cruise. At between three and four thousand, the population nowadays is actually less than it was in the 1850s. But the feel of its heyday as a bustling inland port is still in the air. With the river, the well-but-not over-preserved old buildings and general ambience, we found Argentat more than worth a visit.

*Phylloxera is a microscopic louse or aphid which lives on and in the process kills the roots of grape vines. It destroyed as much as seventy percent of European vineyards in the late 19th century. The dread disease is thought to have been brought to Europe by an American who was collecting vines for his winery in California – said to be the first in the US.

There is no proof of the claim, but it gives the French another very good reason to dislike Americans if not their dollars.

PS. *Although the dictionaries disagree, I have a theory about how we got a common English term from the way the gabares were kept on course. The vessel was steered by a man with a long pole with a vane at the end. This very big and basic sculling device was lashed to a peg in the stern. Two other men with poles would propel and keep the vessel roughly on course, while in the stem or bows a man would wield a long boathook-type pole to push the vessel away from rocks or passing vessels. He was known as the gaffeur. From this (I am guessing) we got not only 'gaffing hook' but also perhaps 'gaffer' as a slang term for the boss in any manual enterprise.*

Whatever the truth, the gaffeur certainly had the riskiest role on board. It was not uncommon for the boathook to become jammed between rocks, depositing the user in the river. The policy then was to leave him to make his own way back to Argentat - if he survived the ducking.

*　　　*　　　*

We decide to take the scenic route through the Valley of the Dordogne and along the 'nut route' from Argentat to the end of our second leg.

This is serious activity holiday territory, and the banks of the river are awash with camps sites and canoe hire businesses. Curiously, the Dordogne seems to have shrunk and become shallower where all the waterborne activity is taking place. Crossing the river to investigate Bassignac-le-Bas, we find it does not live up- or rather down-to its name and the picturesque village looks out over the Dordogne from a considerable height. A sign informs us we may find Bassignac-the-Haut twenty miles upriver, and following the reverse naming logic it will be at risk of flooding when the river is swollen if not actually below the waterline already.

          *   *   *

Our next intended stop is at Collonges la Rouge. Unlike Bassignac-the-Low, it lives up to its name and is very red. This is because the whole village is made from sandstone of that colour.

The guide book informs us that Collonges was built around a priory and was another stop-off point on the Compostela Trail. No modern houses or supermarkets have been allowed to intrude, and the town is thus even more of a tourist magnet than Salers. It is also much more difficult than Salers to find somewhere to park, or to avoid a confrontation with one of the fifty coaches trying to drop off their manifests of mostly aged French passengers. The authorities have quite rightly excluded all traffic from the village, but sited all the car and coach parks in the same place on the main through road. Dogs bark and drivers gesticulate and swear as children play chicken by dashing across the road at the last minute. Old people wander aimlessly about in search of a toilet, and exhaust fumes form a wall of smog. We decide we will explore Collonges at a later date and thoroughly out of season, so pick our way through people and vehicles and kids and dogs and shoot off for the last stopping place in this part of our journey along the Dordogne.

Beaulieu sur Dordogne

We have chosen to end this stage of our journey here because we have done enough for the day, but also because we are on the verge of entering a different world.

Behind us is the under-populated and sometimes gaunt splendour of the Auvergne. Ahead lays a totally different topography and culture, defined by the fairy tale landscape of fortified towns and castles in the air. Another indicator of change are the banana trees beginning to appear at the roadside.

We have also chosen to stop here because of the excellent municipal campsite. It sits beside the river and is in the heart of the town. It is well-run and has a swimming pool and bar. It is also just a half mile stroll from our tent to the centre of the town and a bar which does an excellent steak and frites at a camper-friendly price.

The river is wide and gentle here, and lined in places with medieval buildings. A tourist heartland, there are too many ancient picture-postcard villages in the immediate vicinity to mention.

Originally a small river port called Vellinus, Beaulieu-sur-Dordogne came into prominence in the 9th century when a Benedictine abbey was built on one of the Santiago pilgrims' routes to Spain. In more modern times, the town has become famed for its yearly celebration of a soft fruit. The Strawberry Fair takes place on the second Sunday of May, and the centrepiece is the biggest strawberry flan in All France. Made by a team of local bakers and cake-makers, it measures eight metres across and is topped with eight hundred kilograms of fruit.

Next to our pitch alongside the river, a French family are gathered around a large plastic table. It sags under the weight of plates of meats and cheeses and salads and bottles of water and wine, but the family sit as if attending a funeral. One of the smaller children looks as if she is about to cry, and I think about asking if there is a problem and if we can help. Then, like the sun coming out on a cloudy day, the whole family becomes radiant with delight. One of the boys slips from his seat and runs down the track to where a man is cycling determinedly our way. He stops as the boy arrives, and hands him two large baguettes which were clamped to the back pannier. The boy runs back to the table, waving the loaves in triumph. Obviously, it is the time of the second baking of the day, and the meal could not commence before Papa returned from town with the very freshest of French bread.

We wish them *bon appétit*, erect our tent and then set out for town. Dusk approaches, and although the sun presides over the sylvan setting a gibbous moon waits in the wings as we stop to admire a wild orchard on the river bank. The Dordogne gurgles its pleasure as it makes its never-ending journey to the distant sea. Our steak awaits, and a speciality of the house is to serve the chips anointed with melted camembert. Together with making and baking what may be the biggest strawberry flan in Europe, this small town also dares to serve cheesy chips to visitors. Who says that the French are hidebound in convention when it comes to matters of *haute-cuisine*?

Food and Drink

Dairy farming is not as big in Limousin as elsewhere in France. Perhaps this is why the area is so well-supplied with goat's milk cheeses of distinction. The region favours goats because, as we are told by the marketing boys: The Limousin is a place of forests and plateaux where goats snack on tender foliage and lush grass and mountain flowers to produce milk and then cheese with an inimitable taste.

Well-known varieties include Bi-Caillou, made mainly in the Corrèze department. It is matured for five weeks and the grey rind is sprinkled with yellow flowers. Feuille de Limousin is made in the shape of a chestnut leaf (the symbol of the region) and to qualify for the name, must come from goats with a diet of at least fifty percent of Limousin grass. It also has to be made from raw milk which is untreated and used within 24 hours of milking. Other goaty favourites are Calhada, Calhadons, and Gour Noir, which is coated with fine ash.

Cow's milk cheeses of note include Gouzon and Pas de l'Escalett. This variety is produced in small quantities on the plateau of Larzac, where the pasture is said to impart a taste of mulberry bush and hawthorn to the cheese.

La Tome de Brat is an interesting cheese and made from ewe's milk.

'If chestnuts and turnips ran out, France would be ruined'
(Old Limousin saying)

You cannot travel far in the Limousin without encountering nuts in food or even drink form. In ancient times people here paid their taxes with nuts. There is even an AOC label for Limousin chestnuts, awarded because of their outstanding quality. As well as wonderful chestnut breads, there really are chestnut pâtés, soups, jams, creams, liqueurs, cakes and even, wait for it, a highly-vaunted Limousin Chestnut

Boudin (usually black or white pudding).

Foie gras is everywhere and worth trying in all its different guises if you don't object to how it is produced. Duck is very big in this region, and *Confit de canard* is a signature Limousin dish, often served with chestnuts sautéed in the duck fat in which it was cooked.

So, a pretty typical meal in the Limousin could be:

Cabécou Chaud aux Lards

(When we lived in Normandy, a favourite starter or snack was a round of Camembert on a slice of toasted baguette. We thought we had invented the concept until we travelled south and discovered this tasty dish).

Ingredients

Four slices of smoked pork belly (streaky bacon will do at a push)

Four small rounds of Cabécou (any goat's cheese will do at a push)

Four slices of rustic white bread

Some mixed green salad

A tomato

A shallot

50g crushed walnuts

Some chopped chives

A vinaigrette

Method

Put the slices of pork/bacon on top of the rounds of cheese and put them on the slices of bread.

Put them under the grill.

Meanwhile, arrange your mixed salad and add the chopped shallot and tomato and walnuts and chives.

Put the toasted rounds on top of the bed of salad and drizzle over with a suitable vinaigrette.

Filet Mignon de Porc aux coings

Ingredients

Four quinces

Two tenderloins of pork at roughly 400g a piece

Two chopped onions

A teaspoon of cinnamon

A teaspoon of ginger

A tablespoon of honey

Half a cup of water

Half a cup of dry white wine

Method

Wash and peel the quinces.

Cut into slices and poach for 10 minutes in boiling water, then dry and set aside.

Slice the tenderloins into pieces about 4 centimetres thick.

Fry the onions and add the tenderloins over a strong heat.

When golden brown, add the honey, spices and quinces.

Pour over the water and wine, cover and continue to cook for about half an hour.

Limousin potato pâté *

Many visitors must have wondered why the basic concept of a pie seems mostly unknown in France. Sure we all know about the *en croute* method, but that is invariably puff pastry, all-encompassing and more like a posh sausage roll. However, the Limousin does go for sweet and savoury dishes with pastry lids on. A real winter warmer we have enjoyed was the closest I have seen to a potato pie in this region or any other. It was originally made with leftover dough and cooked in the communal bread oven:

Ingredients (for the pastry)

250g of soft, sifted flour

100g butter

Two eggs

5 g salt

7g fresh baker's yeast

5g castor sugar

4 tbsp warm milk

For the filling:

600g potatoes

150g fatty bacon

Three cloves garlic

One egg yolk (for glazing the pastry)

Some flat-leaved parsley

Some seasoning

Method

Make the dough.
Divide into three.

Mix a third of the softened butter into each portion.

Cover with a tea towel and leave to double in size (usually about an hour) in a warm, draught-free place.

Knead well and reform into one lump and leave for a couple of hours.

Coarsely chop the bacon.

Peel and slice the potatoes.

Butter and flour a deep tart/flan mould.

Line with half the dough.

Put in a layer of potatoes.

Sprinkle over half the chopped bacon, half the finely chopped garlic and half the parsley.

Put on another layer of potatoes and sprinkle on the remaining parsley, garlic and bacon.

Season to taste.

Cover with the remaining pastry and leave to stand while pre-heating the oven to 180°C. (if you do not have a communal bread oven to hand).

Brush the surface of your pâté*/pie with egg yolk.

Cook in oven for an hour.

Limousin purists would serve with a dandelion or lamb's lettuce salad. You may choose otherwise.

*What we generally think of as 'pâté' is what the French would call a terrine or tete. In old French 'pâté' meant 'paste' but was usually applied to a minced meat dish covered with pastry. Or, as we would say, a pie.

Tourtou de Limousin

This very simple Corrèzian favourite is really a pancake made, like Breton crêpes and galettes, with buckwheat flour.

Ingredients

300g buckwheat flour

100g ordinary flour

A packet of yeast

A litre of warm water

Method

Prepare the yeast with a little warm water.

Mix the two flours in a large bowl.

Add the yeast.

Mix well and gradually add the water.

Let stand for 90 minutes in a warm place.

Make small pancakes in a dry hot pan and serve with ice cream or custard.

Walnut Bread

We have talked about the use the denizens of the Limousin make of their award-winning chestnuts, but let us not forget the walnut. It is also used in bread and cakes and all sorts of dishes. The region is also proud of its walnut oil, which is used for dressing but not cooking. Walnut bread is delicious and easy to make, and here's a typical recipe:

Ingredients

300g strong white bread flour

Half a teaspoon of dried yeast

Tablespoon of olive oil

Teaspoon of salt

170ml water

50g shelled and chopped and toasted walnuts

Method

Combine the flour, yeast, salt and walnuts in a bowl.

Make a well and pour in the olive oil.

Add the warmed water.

Make a dough and knead for ten minutes until elastic.

Form into a ball and cover and leave for an hour.

Pre-heat your oven to 200°C.

When it has risen, cook your dough for about half an hour, or when the top is nicely crusty and it sounds hollow when you tap the bottom.

Other regional specialities include clafoutis (cherry pie) and its cousin flognarde, which can be made with any soft fruits. We shall look at some of them at the end of the next leg.

Drink

As in the Auvergne, wine growing in the Limousin has suffered setbacks from disease and rural exodus over the centuries.

It is said that the Romans brought the idea of straw wine to the region in the 3rd century, and the Limousin variety came to national attention because of a passing Saint. St Eloi is the patron saint of horses and had a trick of detaching a leg (of a handy horse) at a time, putting on a shoe and then returning the limb so you could not see the join. In 1622 he was on his way to Rocamadour and stopped off at Vellinus (later to be renamed as the aforementioned BSD), where the locals invited him to sample a particularly well-matured batch of straw wine. He liked it so much that he took several jars to King Dagobert in Paris. The legend has it that the king was so enamoured with the brew that he put his underpants on over his trousers. I am not sure that trousers or underpants were common wear in the 7th century, but it is no more of a tall tale than removing horses' legs to shoe them.

Wine-making on any scale virtually disappeared in the Limousin after the infestation of *phylloxera* in the 19th century, but has emerged in the form of four quality wines. One is *Mille et Une Pierres*, which was highly-prized before the devastation. Nowadays, the Limousin produces a healthy 200,000 bottles of wine a year.

LEG 3

Beaulieu-sur-Dordogne to Souillac

Distance: 70 kilometres

Regions: Limousin, Midi-Pyrénées

Departments: Corrèze, The Lot

The river is getting into its stride as it quits the department of the Corrèze and enters the Lot.

This is one of the original 83 *départéments* created during the Revolution and comes within the Midi-Pyrénées region, which is the largest in France. There is no historical significance to this arbitrary chunk, as it was carved out of a number of old provinces at the end of the last century. According to recent reports, the country may be in line for another re-arrangement.

Francois Hollande has never been the most popular of presidents, but recently hit upon an idea to unite millions of his fellow countrymen and women. The problem is that his scheme could unite those millions against him.

Unveiled in 2014, the proposal was to cut the current tally of regions from 22 to 14. This would see the merging of formerly distinct regions like Upper and Lower Normandy, and the purpose would be to reduce bureaucracy and costs. The re-arrangement, said M. Hollande, would save cash-strapped France €15 billion at almost a stroke. A survey appeared to show that a majority of French people backed the idea, but only it did not affect their region. Another unspoken stumbling block to any geographical simplification would be that, although the French say they hate costly and time-consuming bureaucracy, they relish it…and the more tortuous the better. On that basis, I feel on safe enough ground to predict that the proposals will probably never come to fruition. And, if they do, the result will actually cost more than it was supposed to save.

*   *   *

The thing I like about the castles in this part of the country is that most really live up to usually inaccurate preconceptions about what a proper one should look like. Those here were invariably built in inaccessible, elevated positions to put off potential invaders and literally look down on the locals.

Amongst its peers, the castle at Castelnau-Bretenoux stands out as a real corker. It dates back to at least the 12th century, and stands on a rocky spur overlooking the meeting of two rivers and two regions. Somehow disappointingly, the last owner before the state took over was a Parisian comic opera singer. Whatever its recent provenance, the massive and sheer red slabs of stone glinting in the afternoon sun make it truly intimidating sight.

The further we progress along the castle route, the more it seems as if they are under siege. Though it is not yet fully into the tourist season, tens of thousands of visitors are enjoying the crush. It is a strange aspect of human nature that we are most attracted to the places where we will be most uncomfortable because of the numbers already there.

Ahead of us lay a couple of fine examples:

The gouffre at Padirac

To the French, a gauffre is a sort of waffle, while a *gouffre* is a big hole in the ground. Most know the difference. The hole in the ground we are approaching is really a crowd-puller and coming up for half a million people a year venture into its depths. As we arrive, it looks as if most of them have decided to come today.

A queue stretches back for at least a half mile, and its constituents are surprisingly well-ordered. When they finally get past the ticket office, they will need to descend 75 metres by staircase or lift to enter the cave system. At a hundred metres below ground level, there is a partly-navigable river, and the *gouffre* is acknowledged as one of the most extraordinary phenomena in France. The chasm was created when the roof fell into the vast underground cavern, but I prefer another explanation as to its origins.

Though born in Hungary, St Martin is a French favourite and legends about what he got up to are, well, quite legendary. The one concerning the *gouffre* at Padirac has him and his donkey out and about on the lookout for souls to convert. Then the Devil appeared and hit the ground with his diabolic heel, which opened up a huge hole. He then challenged St Martin to leap across it. The saint made the sign of the cross, spurred the donkey on and the pair soared across the chasm. Proving the veracity of the story, there is an imprint of a donkey's hoof at the edge of the *gouffre*. This story also explains why the vast hole is known as the entrance to Hell.

Rocamadour

Apart from us, renowned personages who have visited our next destination include three kings of France, one of England and a heroine of mine, the Outrageous Eleanor of Aquitaine.

Rocamadour climbs in apparent defiance of gravity up the side of a cliff towering above a tributary to the Dordogne and is named for its founder. St Amadour is the stage name of Zacheus, husband of the woman and later saint who wiped the blood from the face of Jesus during the journey to Calvary. According to legend, Zacheus and Veronica were driven by persecution from Palestine, and set sail on a frail skiff for pastures new. Guided by an angel, they eventually arrived on the coast of Aquitaine. After journeying to Rome and witnessing the martyrdom of St Peter and St Paul, Zacheus returned to France on the death of his wife and built the chapel at what was to become Rocamadour. Miracles began to occur, and in 1166 St Amadour was found in a miraculous state of preservation in a crypt beside the chapel of the Black Virgin*. From then on, Rocamadour became one of the most important pilgrimage destinations in Christendom.

Most visitors nowadays do not follow the tradition of climbing the 216 steps up to the chapel on their knees, but there are walking tours on offer. As well as the Black Virgin, attractions include a bell which rings itself when a miracle occurs at sea, and a fragment of Durandal, the legendary sword of Roland*, which just for good measure is claimed by some to have originally belonged to Hector of Troy.

Statues and paintings of the Virgin Mary with dark skin were not uncommon in medieval Europe, and there are or were fifty in France. A minority group claimed that the Black Madonna actually represented a pagan earth mother, while others claimed she was linked with the Egyptian god Isis.

The cult of the Black Madonna reached its peak in the 13th century, and she became the subject of songs, poems and sagas composed and spread by troubadours. It is around this time that the Holy Grail legends begin, followed by the establishment of the medieval Inquisition, the slaughter of the 'alternative Christian' Cathars, and, a hundred years later, the Knights Templar.

Whatever the true proportion of fact, legend and myth, Rocamadour is a truly remarkable place and comes second only to the Mont St-Michel as France's top tourist attraction.

Around a million and a half people make a pilgrimage to Rocamadour each year, and I have to confess that we were not amongst their number on this visit. From across the valley we used a telescope to spy on the hundreds of cars and coaches and thousands of people laying siege to Rocamadour, and beat a retreat after agreeing to return at a quieter time.

What I couldn't sort out about the shrine at Rocamadour was whether the effigy was meant to be of the Virgin Mary and made of walnut that just turned black with time, or that the makers actually meant to represent a Madonna who was black.

Roland was a Frankish military leader of the 8th century who features largely in the collection of literary work and legend known as The Matter of France. His heroic story is told in the 11th-century Song of Roland. His enchanted sword Durendal was said to be unbreakable, and owed its magical powers to four sacred relics within the hilt. They were a tooth once belonging to St Peter, the blood of St Basil, strands of hair from St Denis...and a piece of a robe worn by the Virgin Mary. Durendal (from the old French 'to endure') was believed to have been forged by legendary Norse armourer Wayland the Smith, and given by an angel to Charlemagne for presentation to Roland. It is said that a fragment of the obviously not unbreakable sword is wedged in a wall in the village of Rocamadour, but the tourist office (surprisingly) have declared it a fake.

*   *   *

In France, it is permissible to pee, break wind and even make love in the open. Eating on the move is strictly infra-dig, and the rules are quite inviolable.

In spite of this, the French have turned eating and drinking in the open into an art form, and *le picnic* may take place in the oddest locations. I have seen elaborate meals being taken in cemeteries, car parks, other people's gardens and even on the hard shoulders of motorways. Although constantly challenged by young people, eating on the hoof is still frowned upon. This is why you find so little litter in the form of sweet wrappings and half-eaten sandwiches on the highways and byways of France. In Britain, of course, people cannot get from A to B without putting something in their mouths. On motorways I have seen drivers in the outer lane with a mobile phone in one hand and a cheese roll in the other. Not so here.

It is okay to consume an ice cream or *croque monsieur* (toasted cheese and ham sandwich) in the open air, but only in the environs of where it was bought. You may snack outside a snack bar, but not walk away from the point of purchase before finishing it.

Today we have broken that covenant, and are paying the price.

We were hot, dusty and sweaty after queuing up in the searing heat to not visit Rocamadour, and my wife suggested an ice cream or lolly would be in order. The concept of a brightly liveried van which plays a snatch of *Greensleeves* every ten minutes being unknown in France, we dropped in to a handy convenience store and bought a box of Magnum Originals.

Sitting in a park under the shadow of an ancient yew tree, we broke open the box and unwrapped two ice creams on a stick. Within minutes, word had spread and a small crowd gathered. Children nudged each other, pointed and giggled. Old maids enjoyed the opportunity to become righteously outraged, and one woman swept up her tiny dog and hurried away with her hand over its eyes.

By the time we had finished and put the wrappers in our pockets for later disposal (waste bins in public places are another virtually unknown concept in France) there was a sense that the crowd was turning ugly, so we pushed our way through and made off in the car. As we rejoined the main road my wife said she could hear a siren approaching fast. Either there had been an accident nearby, or the police were on their way to investigate a couple of foreigners causing an outrage to public decency in the Parc Charles De Gaulle.

Martel

Martell is one of the oldest brandy-making houses in France, founded in 1715 in Cognac by Jean Martell.

Despite the missing 'l' and to the surprise of some visitors, Jean and his products have nothing to do with the Martel in the Lot. I suspect that the tourist authorities do not trouble to correct the understandable mistake, and we met half a dozen tourists who were looking in vain for any references to the family and its business.

Actually, Martel is distinguished for its long history and selection of impressive old buildings, including seven large towers. Another distinction is that, If she is still there, the lady who served us tea in the PMU is in the running for my award for the national Rudest Bar Person Award. As we are in France, this is a sometimes fiercely contested competition.

Although it had some walls thrown up as a defence against invading Brits in the Hundred Years War, Martel did not begin life as a military defence post. Trade has always been the *raison d'etre* for the town, sitting as it did on the Paris -Toulouse trading route. There is a busy market here twice a week, specialising in truffles in December. On the evening we arrived, the Place de la Halle was occupied with what looked like a strange convocation of dodgy undertakers and representatives from the ranks of the Undead.

Milling around under the covered market were dozens of middle-aged men, mostly dressed in short, closely fitting black overcoats, black trousers and shoes. They also wore black wide-brimmed fedora hats which did not sit well with the rest of their ensemble or their general age and demeanour. Thankfully, only a minority of the wearers sported lank pony-tails. From a distance it seemed that some of the older men were badly bowed under the weight of their years, but then we saw that their stooped stance was a result of the enormous Del-Boy golden medallions slung round their necks.

As we got nearer, we saw an even stranger figure flitting amongst the group. In spite of his advanced years, the tall and cadaverously thin man had jet black hair oiled and scraped back to reveal a marked widow's peak. He had a deathly white pallor but cherry-red lips. No medallions for him, and instead of the overcoat he was wearing a white bow tie, tails and a long black cape which flapped sinisterly in his wake.

I asked someone in the small knot of spectators what was going on, and he looked at me as if it were all perfectly obvious. Obviously, we were witnessing the closing moments of an induction ceremony for new members of an association for the Admiration of the Truffle. The new members had gone through a rigorous course of instruction and examination, and had been found worthy to join the exclusive club.

What made today's event so special was that all such ceremonies were traditionally held after dark, and this was the first time the Grand Master has appeared in daylight.

I open my mouth to ask if he has ever been seen to buy garlic in the local *épicerie* or adjust his dress in a mirror, but my wife shoots me a warning look and drags me off in search of a bar with a friendly waitress.

Souillac

At first sight, Souillac seems to have a slightly edgy side to its character.

The main through road is like any other, but there are some interestingly louche side roads with unusual shops and people sitting outside on rickety chairs or lounging in the doorways. Male Souillacans with lots of facial hair and gaunt features stand face-to-face, clutching carrier bags and cigarettes and holding what appear to be vitally important conversations at close quarters.

It is a universal rule of street life that some people with plenty of time on their hands tend to speak and move very quickly considering that they have nowhere to be or go. They also like to stand very close to the person they are talking with, speaking in a low, urgent tone as if discussing matters of great import. Most are probably discussing last night's telly or where to go for the first drink of the day, but it looks as if they are discussing a potential bank job.

Like Martel, Souillac lies on the old Toulouse-Paris trading route. Once it was ringed by a wall with five gates, but that did not stop it getting knocked about a good bit during the wars which raged in this area through the centuries. There are enough striking medieval buildings surviving to give the town a feel of its past, and at coming up for four thousand inhabitants, it can support a good few bars and eating places.

The population of any proposed stopping-off place is always of interest to us, as it is an invariable indication of what you can expect to find there in the way of facilities and commercial premises. In the low hundreds you will be lucky to find a bar or shop, though there will always be at least two hairdressing salons. Anywhere that a thousand people or so call home will be able to supports a variety of bars, a licensed betting shop (PMU), a couple of convenience stores, a supermarket and at least four hairdressing establishments. Even bigger towns will boast a variety of foreign restaurants and at least one, usually pathetic, Irish bar. The final invariable rule is that an indicator of an 'edgy' town with a busy nightlife is related to the number of kebab shops. If they outnumber the hairdressing salons, keep your hand on your wallet while out after dark.

After studying the guide book and making several enquiries, we find that the tourist office at Souillac is hidden away in the back of a church. The interior is all plate glass and dressed stone and minimalistic works of art, which is a bad sign. Another general rule about tourist offices in France is that the degree of arty-fartyness in its style and location will be in direct opposition to the level of service and interest you'll get from the people working there. Whether they mean it or not, it usually seems that they don't want people - especially scruffy foreigners - messing up the place. Again in inverse proportion, the more lived-in and even chaotic a tourist office is, the friendlier and more helpful service you are going to get.

On duty when we arrived via the plate glass doors was a very large young lady, sitting at a spindly desk and pretending to be busy on her keyboard. Finally, she looked up and took a sudden and somewhat histrionic intake of breath.

I checked my zip, then realised she had probably taken against my home-made shorts. They were made from a pair of trousers I was given in the 1970s when loons were all the rage. Loons were the natural descendants of Oxford bags of the 30s, and differed from flared trousers by being even wider and maintaining the vast width all the way up to the crutch. Since their conversion into knee-length shorts, my shorts have grown rigid and can actually stand on their own. A significant advantage is that the stiffness and extraordinary leg width ensures cooling air circulation on the hottest days. I do not mind the attention they attract, and it has been the basis of many an interesting conversation I would otherwise probably never have had. However, the legs tend to retain their full circumference when I am seated, which means I have to take care if facing a female diner of apparent sensitive nature. It can also be hard to enter some buildings without turning sideways. This was the case with the fancy glass door leading in to the tourist bureau at Souillac.

When we asked about a campsite or a budget hotel, the young woman gave a look that said her suspicions about the sort of people she was dealing with had been confirmed. Nettled and suspecting the reaction I would get, I made matters worse by asking if there was a decent Indian curry house or Chinese restaurant in town.

After rocking back in shock, the lady did another sharp intake of breath and pantomimed round-eyed astonishment before asking why we have come to France if we do not want to eat French food. I said that when we are in China we do not eat only Chinese food. Then there is the fact that Britain had a much larger empire than France, and so we Brits probably had more developed and adventurous tastes in food.

*   *   *

French camp sites are like hotels in that the star rating and overnight rate do not give much of a clue to the ambience and level of service. In fact and a bit like the paradox of tourist offices, we have generally experienced more bad service, disdain, lack of interest and even hostility from grand hotels with four-star ratings than shabby ones with two or less. Perhaps the stars actually represent the level of hauteur the receptionists can summon up.

Whether or not this is true, the general rule seems to apply to the *Verte Rive* campsite at Souillac. As it is so early in the season, much work is in progress but behind the pile of rubble at the gate we are given a really warm welcome by a beautiful young woman. Delphine tells us she and her husband and mother have only owned the site since the spring so do not know what a summer may bring. Perhaps, I think as she shows us round, not having had a full season of dealing with campers is why she is still so helpful and friendly.

Old hands at the game, we find the site more than meets our criteria. Apart from the relaxed manner of our hostess, the Verte Rive is a good way from the road and lives up to its claim of being literally on the banks of the Dordogne. Moules and chips are always on the menu at the bar, and when I ask about last orders for food and drink, Delphine looks puzzled. As long as there is a customer, she says, the bar stays open.

It looks like rain, so we decide to splash out on a caravan for the night. There is one right by the river and we can have it at less than the usual rate, says Delphine. This may be because it needs a bit of work done, or because I have already casually mentioned that I am a travel writer.

We move in and I receive only a slight shock from the light switch before heading for the bar. On arrival we meet the couple's little daughter. She is cuddling what I at first take to be a teddy bear, then see is a live cockerel. His name, Enola tells me solemnly, is Rock 'n' Roll.

*   *   *

We have eaten and drunk very well for very little money, and decide to take a look at the river before turning in. As we walk through the trees, I reflect on how we could have gone elsewhere and missed meeting this lovely family and their burgeoning business. But then, it is possible if not likely that we could have found an even better place. Life is full of what-ifs, and it is probably for the best we cannot know what would have happened had we taken another course.

The river flows by, dark and swift and shallow. There is a full moon, and it reflects on the metal sides of a punt-like vessel being borne swiftly along by the flow. On board are two men, dressed in the standard jungle warfare military outfits. One is using a pole to keep the craft on course and away from rocks or too-shallow water. The other is kneeling in the bows, holding a powerful lantern aloft. Whether he is looking for fish or submerged dangers I do not know, but the scene makes a striking tableau as they sweep past.

Donella has brought glasses and some local cheese, and I have brought a beer bottle holding Delphine's special house drink, which is a very different sort of Kir. We settle down for a nightcap and as the river continues its endless journey, I think again what a lucky man I am.

Food & Drink

Whilst meandering through the Lot we've also been dipping in to the Midi-Pyrénées, which is the largest region in France. There are two departments with the word 'Lot' in them in the region, namely the Lot itself (46), and the Lot et Garonne (47). To confuse matters further, the two *départéments* were formed after the Revolution from the old province of Quercy, and folk like to hang on to that name. This is one of the least-populated parts of France, with only 31 human inhabitants sharing every square kilometres of the Lot.

As we have learned, cattle as well as people can be a bit thin on the ground in this part of France, so cheese made from goat's milk dominates. Rocamadour belongs to the Cabécous family and has a smooth, nutty flavour.

There are certainly more geese and ducks than people in the Lot, and they are put to good use in regional recipes like this simple but delicious salad:

Salade Quercynoise

Ingredients

Some frisée and mesclun salad*

12 cherry tomatoes

100g shelled walnuts

250g confit of duck gizzards, thinly sliced

200g foie gras

A tablespoon of balsamic vinegar

A tablespoon of vegetable oil

A tablespoon of walnut oil

Method

Sautée the gizzards over a medium heat, then make up your salad with them, the leaves, tomatoes and walnuts and chunks of fois gras.

Finally, sprinkle the lot with the vinegar, lemon juice and walnut oil dressing.

NB. This hearty starter goes well with walnut bread (*see the previous Food & Drink section*).

Mesclun is nothing more than a mixture of young salad leaves, and the idea originated in Provence. Frisée is also known as curly endive and is a form of chicory often used in mesclun.

Far au Choux

This is a Quercy speciality which comes under puddings, but of the savoury sort. It employs basically the same batter as used for crêpes or our own Yorkshire pudding, and other vegetables can be used for the filling. It is normally served as a starter.

Ingredients

A cabbage

100g all-purpose flour

2 large eggs

A cup of milk (250 ml)

A tablespoon of rendered duck or goose fat

Method

Remove the outer coarse leaves of the cabbage, core, chop.

Cook in boiling salted water for five minutes, then drain.

Heat your oven to 220°C.

Whisk the flour, eggs and milk into a stiff batter and add the cabbage pieces.

Season well with salt and pepper.

Grease a suitable high-sided oven dish or cast iron frying pan and put in the oven till the fat is literally smoking.

Stir the batter and cabbage mix, then pour into the dish and bake for around half an hour or until your pudding is swollen and brown without burning.

Aligot

Cheesy potatoes is the sort of creation that most of us would associate with an offering in a British caff rather than a French delicacy. In fact, Aligot is a firm favourite throughout the south-west and is as simple to make as it is delicious to eat. The original recipe calls for Cantal cheese, but if this too costly or rare, experiment with a British variety like Cheddar. Personally, I have difficulty in distinguishing fully mature Cantal from the king of English cheeses.

Ingredients

450g of King Edward or Desirée potatoes

A big clove of peeled and chopped garlic

25g of butter

250g of grated Cantal cheese

Salt and pepper

Method

Put the garlic and butter in a pan on a very low heat.

Peel the potatoes and cut into smallish cubes.

Sprinkle the cubes with salt and steam for around half an hour.

Use a hand whizzer to start to break up the potato, gradually introducing the garlic, butter and cheese.

Stuffed Quercy Pigeons

As in the Auvergne, *pigeonniers* are part of the landscape of the Lot. They are a bird which has gone out of food fashion on our side of the Channel, but this dish is perennially popular in the province:

Ingredients

Two pigeons, dressed

100g walnuts

100g sultanas

An egg

A cup of breadcrumbs

A clove of garlic

A teaspoon of runny honey

Juice and rind of a lemon

Some olive oil

Some butter

Some parsley

Seasoning

Method

Carefully fry the garlic in some butter, then add 100ml of water, boil, add the sultanas and simmer for a few moments before draining.

Toast the walnuts and combine with the breadcrumbs, half the sultanas, the beaten egg, half the chopped parsley, some olive oil and lemon juice and seasoning.

Stuff the birds.

Put the birds in a deep roasting pan and sprinkle some olive oil over. Dot with butter and place in a pre-heated oven

(200°C) for half an hour or until golden brown.

Glaze the birds with the honey, pour over the sultana mixture and garnish with the parsley.

Gabure Gersoise

Gabure is a real winter-warmer Gascon favourite, and in essence is a ham and vegetable stew. Gabure Gersoise is a thick cabbage, white bean and duck confit soup which is a meal in itself.

Ingredients

Two legs of duck confit

Four ounces of diced bacon

Six cloves of minced garlic

A large carrot, chopped

A thinly sliced onion

A small leek

Half a cup of dry white wine

Six cups of chicken stock

A cup of dried cannellini beans, soaked overnight

A sprig of parsley

A sprig of thyme

Some black pepper

A teaspoon of juniper berries

A bay leaf

A small Savoy cabbage, cored and thinly sliced

A peeled russet potato, cubed

A small turnip, peeled and cubed

Some salt and pepper

Method

Cook the duck legs in a big pan until the fat is rendered and the flesh soft (about ten minutes).

Shred the meat, discarding the bone and set aside.

Fry bacon in pan until crisp then set aside.

Add garlic, onion, carrot and leek and cook till golden.

Add wine and boil.

Reduce liquid to half.

Add beans and stock and return to boil.

Put herbs and peppercorns into a cheesecloth bag and add to pan.

Cook for an hour or so until beans are tender.

Add potato and cabbage and turnip and seasoning and cook until tender.

Stir in duck and bacon pieces.

Gâteau à la Broche

This is (to say the least) a very unusual Midi-Pyrénées speciality, served often as a wedding cake or for other celebrations. Just one of the reasons it is unusual is that it is traditionally cooked over an open fire rather than in an oven. The recipe and method are said to have been brought back by Napoleon's troops from the Balkans, and the procedure involves putting the mix *on* rather than in to a mould and turning it on a spit. It is said a good Gâteau à la Broche requires up to twenty layers of cake mix and can weigh in at up to five kilograms. It is far too complicated and demanding to make without the skills, patience and kit, but this is what the French call the easy way. Good luck:

NB. If you make it full size to this monster formula, be sure to invite plenty of friends round to share it with.

The kit

A cone of hardwood, reaching to a height of 45 cms, 15cm at the base.

Some greaseproof paper

Some string

A rotisserie with commodious drip tray

An open fire

Ingredients

A kilogram of sugar

A kilogram of flour

A kilogram of butter

24 eggs

Two packets sugar vanilla

Two packets yeast

A pinch of salt

Four tablespoons of rum

Method

Separate the yolks and white of the eggs.

Beat the yolks with the sugar.

Add the rum, salt, vanilla sugar and butter.

Gently fold in the sifted flour, yeast and stiffly beaten egg whites.

Leave to stand for an hour.

Wrap your mould in the greaseproof paper and assemble over the fire.

Get a friend to gently turn the spit while you ladle batter on to the mould.

Continue until you have used up all the batter.

Rescue the drippings (or cascades) from the drip tray and start again until you have a lovely 'pimply' gâteau.

Allow to cool before cutting up and sharing.

Drink

Most of the wine-growing action in the Lot happens on 4000 hectares in and around the capital, Cahors. The tradition of viticulture goes back to Roman times, but it was the marriage of Eleanor of Aquitaine to Henri Plantagenet in 1152 that kicked off a period of intense growth. The 'black wine'* grown there became the must-have brand, and by the early years of the 14th century, Quercy (of which Cahors was the provincial capital) accounted for more than half of all exports from Bordeaux.

Punitive taxes incurred by the Hundred Years War and plain jealousy from the viticulturists of Bordeaux sent the region's wine trade into a slow decline, and the death knell was the arrival of the dreaded phylloxera.

It was not until the middle of the 20th century that Cahors made a comeback with the re-introduction of the Malbec grape.

A specialty *aperitif* peculiar to this part of France is *Fénelon*, which is a mixture of red wine, walnut liqueur and cassis.

The term 'black wines' is used because it is said you should not be able to see through a good glass of Cahors red. Some growers say you should be able to stand a knife up in it, and a local custom (faire chabrot) is to slop a smidgeon into your bowl at the end of a meal and see it off 'like a goat.'

Kir Delphine

This is the very localised noggin we had at the campsite in Souillac. In case you did not know, Kir is a popular *aperitif* named for a Burgundian mayor who thought it a good idea to mix white wine with a slug of blackcurrant liqueur (*crème de cassis*). A number of varieties on the theme evolved, including cassis with Champagne (Kir Royale) and my favourite, Kir Normand, which replaces the wine with sparkling cider.

The version we tried at the campsite at Souillac was purely the invention of our hostess. A word of warning if you try it: The French excel at coming up with enamel-stripping concoctions, and it is advisable to have a toothbrush handy for immediate use after trying a glass of Delphine's Delight:

Ingredients

A bottle of sparkling wine

Some lychee syrup

A large spoonful of cane sugar

Some Grenadine

Some Pulco*

Method

Put a shot of grenadine in a suitable glass, add the lychee syrup and sugar. Top up the glass with very cold wine, then dribble the Grenadine in to colour the mix. Finally, take a sip and add Pulco till the mixture is as sweet or tart as you want.

In Wales, Pulco is the name of a Welsh folk artist. In France it is the name of a very popular and expensive lemon juice. As I said earlier, the French do like mixing alcohol with all sorts of unusual fruit juices and concentrates.

LEG 4

Souillac to
la Roque-Gageac

Distance: 35 kilometres

Regions: Midi-Pyrénées, Aquitaine

Departments: The Lot, The Dordogne

Domme

After doing some research in roadside bars, I find we are approaching a part of an ancient bit of France which was one of the world's first example of colour coding.

As far as I can make out, the Périgord is a former province conforming roughly in size and shape with the current Dordogne department. There are or were four Périgords, each named for a colour with which it was associated in some way. Thus Périgord Noir was so called because of its black truffles, while Périgord Blanc (the middle bit) was named for the white rocks to be found there. Périgord Vert lies to the north and was so called because of the greenery of the landscape, and Périgord Pourpre honoured the colour of its purple grapes. As touched on earlier, the region has strong connections with the Knights Templar and was much fought over in the Hundred Years War, explaining the number of castles and fortified towns here.

With its connection with the Cathars and Knights Templar and at the heart of the Holy Grail legends, it is a fascinating part of a fascinating country, and we shall look at its heritage in more detail at a later stage.

*   *   *

We are following a minor road, flirting with the river as we pass through a series of mostly pretty villages. Change is almost literally in the air as our westward route takes us away from the Lot and towards the department of the Dordogne and fairytale castle territory.

This is the land of the *bastide*, which broadly means a fortified village or town in a high place. There are seven hundred of them in France, mostly in the south-west. Ironically, they now attract millions of Britons a year, but were put in place mostly to keep us out.

In the 13th century much of the south of France was in

the hands of the English, and the hilltop fortifications were an attempt to draw a line. Some of the *bastide* in the Dordogne are nothing short of spectacular and few more so than our next destination.

Domme ticks all the boxes for a tourist magnet and is proudly referred to by the French (or so the publicity blurb goes) as The Acropolis of Périgord. I can't really see the similarity except that they are both built in high places, but Domme is certainly a pleasure to the eye.

The small but perfectly formed town is set high above the river at the top of a corkscrew road, setting it apart from the modern world. Unlike most *bastide* towns, its walls and gateways are still intact. 'Stunning' is a word regularly done to death in guides and books like this one, but I reckon the views from the ramparts would knock a particularly insensitive elephant out. There is even a grotto beneath the town. Apart from these attractions, I am also looking forward to our visit because the town and I go back a long way.

I first visited Domme in the 1960s, when hitchhiking my way down to the south coast. Nobody had warned me that this bit of France is quite hilly and (in those days) cars were a rarity in the most isolated areas. On my massive yomp I often felt I had passed through some sort of rift in the space-time continuum, and I was certainly a curiosity in this part of the country at that time. Believe it or not, people would come out of their homes to look at me as I passed through the more remote villages.

Thirty years later, my wife and I found ourselves in Domme one dark and stormy winter night, though we only found out where we were after we got there. We also had the best accidental meal we have ever had in France. I wrote about our visit a few years later, and this is what I said:

We were on our way to visit friends in the deep south, and as usual I had underestimated the journey time. I had also overestimated the availability of accommodation in the depths of winter. Some hours earlier we had passed a seedy bar on the outskirts of what looked like the location for the shooting of The Village of the Damned, and my wife had suggested we stop and make the best of it.

In a sulk I refused. As per our marital agreement, I had blamed her poor navigation, though it had been my idea to go by the scenic route rather than stay on the motorway. Now, dusk was falling, and we were on a lonely road in a strange and increasingly desolate place. I was still in denial that we were lost, even after my wife pointed out an interesting rock formation which looked ominously similar to one we had passed an hour before. Irritatingly, all the names on the map seemed to end with 'ac', but none of them agreed with the road signs we occasionally passed.

Then it began to snow, the road narrowed, and the signs petered out altogether. The petrol gauge had been hovering on zero for some time, and I was promising Victor the Volvo anything if he would just last out till we arrived at the next service station. Without doubt, the situation was getting serious. Then, just as my wife said she thought she could hear a wolf howling, we emerged from a pass between two gigantic slabs of rock and saw civilisation.

There on a hilltop was the brooding outline of an ancient town, its grim walls and towers standing out against the silvery night sky. As far as I could see at this range, there were no large bats circling the battlements or villagers with flaming torches laying siege to the keep, so in our situation the place looked almost welcoming. And it was only a mile away. At least, it was only a mile away as the bat flies. As we crawled upwards in an ever decreasing spiral, the road got narrower, the snow fell with ever increasing intensity, and the precipice alongside the road got steeper.

Then as Victor was beginning to fight for breath and I was contemplating ending our misery with a quick wrench on the steering wheel, we reached the end of the corkscrew climb. Limping through a giant stone archway and in to the cobbled square, we found the town to be apparently abandoned. Although in familiar France, we seemed to be in another, stranger and certainly darker world. Either we had entered a different dimension immediately after leaving the motorway, or the entire community were at a goat-sacrificing ceremony in the next town.

After making a crude crucifix from my car jack and lever, I led the way through the empty streets. Eventually, we saw a single light, dimly filtering through the closed shutters of a gaunt stone building. An old van stood outside, and there were steps up to a pair of double doors, and what looked like the outline of a human body on a faded sign above the entrance. Either it was an hotel or the town mortuary. Looking at each other and the desolated streets and snow-filled sky, we silently considered our alternatives and entered.

Inside, we found a huge vaulted room with flagged floor, a cat with three legs, several trestle tables and a selection of customers who looked at us as if they had run out of goats for next week's coven meeting. Crossing the floor to the sound of our own footsteps, we smiled weakly, and I tried not to look for a bolt through the giant barman's neck when I ordered our drinks.

As I spoke, the muttered conversation in the room ceased, and the atmosphere became, if possible, even colder. Unable to summon up the nerve to ask about accommodation, I led the way to a corner seat, put my back to the wall and started drawing up an escape plan. We had always sought out unusual places to stay during our trips around France, but this was beyond the pale. Swiftly finishing our drinks, we got up, and staying close together, sidled back to the bar to pay.

As I debated waiting for the change or making a break for it while his attention was diverted, I saw the barman frowning at the money I had given him and realised it was a twenty pound note. Holding it up to the light, he looked at it and then me, and asked suspiciously if we were English. Thinking quickly, I explained that I was actually more than half-Scottish on my father's side, and my wife's mother came from Wales. In our travels I find that this is usually the safest bet in a strange and hostile setting, as to my knowledge neither Scotland nor Wales has ever colonised, occupied or been at war with any foreign power except the English. However, the way things were going, this could be the one town in Europe invaded and conquered by an away team from the Cameron Highlanders.

For a moment, the giant scratched his head where his left ear should have been while he looked us up and down, then bared his teeth in what could just have been a smile. From then on, the atmosphere was to change dramatically. Our new friend barked a few words at the customers, gave me back my banknote and asked us if we had anywhere to stay for the night. As we relaxed over another drink, he explained that my size and our strange accents had given the impression that we were Germans. Every man in the bar had lost a relative to local atrocities during the war, he went on, and return visits from the Bosche were not exactly encouraged.

Hearing we were lost, he insisted that we stay for the night, and shortly showed us up to a surprisingly comfortable room. Hungry but at least having found shelter for the night, we were preparing to go to bed when a heavy knocking rattled the solid oak door in its frame. Opening it tentatively, I was confronted with a man who looked like the barman's bigger and uglier brother. He was dressed in grimy chef's whites, and more importantly, carrying a large cleaver. As I began to babble that we had never even visited Germany, he interrupted me to tetchily enquire if we were coming down for the gourmet evening. There were only two seats left, and the aperitifs would be served in exactly twelve minutes.

We were downstairs in less than five, and found the bar transformed. The trestle tables had been dressed with white linen tablecloths, and the customers and cat had obviously gone to the goat barbecue. In their place, a throng of smartly dressed diners were sitting in obvious anticipation of the treat to come. Hurriedly, we found our places and joined them.

Over the next three hours, our taste sensors were to be transported to Paradise. I am the first to agree with my wife that I am a gourmand rather than a gourmet, but even I could tell that we were in the presence of an eating experience as unique as our surroundings. There were a full five courses, each accompanied by a different wine, and each based upon a central theme of the fruits of the local streams, fields and forests. There were mushrooms the size of parasols, and cheek of wild boar with a skin that crackled and echoed around the hall like gunshot fire when bitten into. There was hare, trout and other mysterious animal titbits which I relished, but chose not to have identified by our ever-attentive waiter. There were even five different textures and types of local bread, some stuffed with crisp golden nuggets of walnut.

After each course came an oral examination, conducted by the giant chef, who visited every table after each course to demand frank comment on his offerings. He said he would equally accept praise and constructive criticism, and it was a mark of the quality of the meal that not a single diner complained or even made a helpful suggestion for future reference. In my experience, this is almost unheard of in France, even with a meal of those standards. I like to think it was because our table could not find a single thought as to how the feast could have been enhanced, but it might have had a little to do with the fact that our chef de cuisine was still carrying his cleaver.

Next day, the snow lay deep and crisp and fairly even upon the cobbles of the square as we drove contentedly through the giant archway. Reaching the road at the bottom of the hill and heading back to civilisation, we swore that we would return one day.

If only, that is, we would ever be able to find the place again.

Back to the present and we find that though the fabric of Domme has changed little, the town seems to have appointed a PR company since our last visit. Signs along the route announce that it is market day, and everyone in the region seems to want to attend.

Unable to escape if we chose to, we join a queue of cars inching up the corkscrew road as joggers overtake us and skinny cyclists with their arses in the air zoom past with obvious relish.

At the top of the hill we find the cause of the logjam. An impressively fat policeman is on arm-waving duty and fulfilling his remit to make the situation worse. So, we have plenty of time to take in the scene as we follow the mini-train through the square. The ancient market place is filled with people and upmarket stalls selling things at twice the price they would fetch in a less elevated situation. Sometimes it is more than double the price in Super U. I note that the asking price for an elaborately plaited string of garlic hanging from a very twee stall would probably have bought a week's groceries in the not-so-distant past. As I wind the window down and try to find a place to park, I hear gratingly familiar voices and realise that most of the people queuing up to pay through their noses for a bit of fruit and veg are fully-paid up members of our chattering classes.

The women wear huge sunglasses and ridiculously wide-brimmed straw hats they fondly imagine are of the type once worn by peasants in the vineyards. Dresses and scarves are uniformly diaphanous and float in the wake of the wearers, some of whom would outweigh the rotund Gendarme. Elsewhere, braying voices entreat Cassandras, Sophies and Olivers not to pick their noses or cast themselves off the rampart walls.

We pass the sweating policeman for the third time before giving up the search and head for the corkscrew descent. Perhaps we will come back in the winter to get a real taste of Domme, or perhaps like so much of deep France, what we found all those years before has gone forever.

Sarlat-le-Caneda

We are leaving the river to its own devices as we head north-west to see if Sarlat-le-Caneda is all it is cracked up to be. Hopefully it will not be market day and we will be able to find a place to park.

Situated in the Périgord Noir, Sarlat owes its fame to have been left mostly untouched by passing times and fancies, and is said to be the town most representative of the 14th century in all France.

Amongst other activities and spectacles, Sarlat offers a mammoth Christmas fair, a celebration of the truffle in January, and a goose festival in February. As it is June, none of these events are taking place, and something else must be responsible for the town being a no-go area. We look at the mass of humanity swarming the streets and the gridlock traffic, then look at each other and in silent agreement decide we will return on another, quieter day.

*   *   *

Although the river lies to our south, we are travelling northwards into the greenest part of Périgord. Having come this far away from the river and failing to break into Sarlat, we are pressing on to one of the most ancient dwelling places in Europe.

According to my brochure, a team of potholers from the deliciously named Périgueux Spelunking Club were following their hobby in 1953 when they literally stumbled upon a previously unknown cavern. The giant grotto spread for 13 kilometres on several levels, and held a treasure which was not discovered for another five years. A series of prehistoric painting were eventually uncovered, and now the Grotte de Villars offers its visitors the chance to see and wonder at art created 17,000 years ago. Or in our case, not to even see.

Arriving a-tremble to see the incredibly ancient

representations of horses, bison and even a human being, we join a throng of schoolchildren and get to within a metre of the entrance before being weeded out by a middle-aged lady who appears to have been sucking on a lemon shortly before our meeting. If I am not mistaking her, she says that, unless we are a part of the school group, we cannot enter the grotto. I apologise for our tagging on behind the party, and explain that it is a strange British tradition called queuing. Wincing as if my accent is causing her physical injury, the lady says it is not a question of whether or not we are queuing. If we are not-pre-booked, we cannot go in to see the wonders of the grotto and wall paintings. I force a smile and say that we have come several hundred miles to visit the site and suggest we pre-book for later in the day. The lady's lips almost appear again as she smiles a very thin smile and says this is very much not possible. At this time of year the grotto is open only to organised groups, and in spite of my size, she does not think I can qualify as a group.

*   *   *

Having been thwarted of our plans to visit two Périgordian attractions, we are on our way to try for success at a third.

Retreating from our encounter with the guardian of the grotto, we were heading back towards the river when I spotted a faded roadside sign announcing the presence of a Templar's Chapel in the vicinity. An arrow points down a lane off the main road, so we follow it.

The Order of the Knights Templar and its members and exploits have spawned hundreds of books and thousands of stories, some of them well beyond the realms of the even faintly credible. The legends involve links with freemasonry, vast treasures still awaiting discovery, and even the Holy Grail, depending on your interpretation of what the Holy Grail is.

The basic facts are that the Order was formed at the beginning of the12th century, after the First Crusade and when a French nobleman enlisted eight of his knightly relatives. Broadly, their mission was to protect pilgrims on their way to holy places. The group approached the king of Jerusalem, who allowed them to set up shop at the Temple Mount, one of the most revered sites to Judaism, Islam and Christianity. The small band of brothers named themselves as The Poor Fellow Soldiers of Christ and of the Temple of Solomon, shortly shortened to Knights Templar. Those wanting to enter at the highest level of the Order were required to be of noble birth and to swear vows of obedience, chastity, poverty and piety. This changed as huge donations poured in and the richest and perhaps craftiest members went into banking as well as fighting the good fight.

By the beginning of the 14th century, the Templars had become a vastly rich and powerful body, even considering forming its own state in the south-east of France. This, together with the facts that they paid no taxes and were owed a huge amount of money by the Crown understandably worried King Philip. At dawn on Friday the 13th of October, 1307, leading Templars were rounded up and imprisoned on trumped-up charges, including devil-worship. After torture, most of the Knights confessed and were executed. The Order was dissolved by the Pope in 1312, but the legends left behind grew with the telling. Along with stories of vast treasures hidden in France and elsewhere, it became a popular belief that the order had discovered and secreted the cup used by Christ during the Last Supper.

Others thought the Holy Grail was not a cup, but some artefact or secret which would rock the foundations of Christianity. The direct link between the Templars and the Dordogne was Armand de Périgord, elected Grand Master of the Order in 1232. Whatever the truth about the wealth, activities and secrets of the Knights Templar, they continue to engender world-wide interest and fascination. Indeed in this land of castles and legend, their presence seems almost palpable.

*　　　*　　　*

Unfortunately for us, any secrets contained in this Templar's chapel will remain unsolved, as the doors are locked.

The ancient but unremarkable little building sits in a field, and it appears the inside is undergoing a programme of internal restoration in preparation for the tourist season. As with food, the French are rigid with their parameters. A waiter will faint if you order red wine with fish, and holidays take place when offices, factories and Paris empty for the month of August.

There is a dusty window above my head at the back of the chapel, and to get a glimpse of the inside I climb on to one of a pile of stone blocks and peer through a dusty window. I see nothing more exciting than a scaffolding tower and some tools, and it is only when I climb down that my wife points out I have been standing not on a stone block, but a stone coffin.

One of the things we like about the French is that they tend not to worry too much about where they leave things. In England, the handful of ancient and historically significant stone coffins would have been locked away or put on show behind glass; here, they lay higgledy-piggeldly alongside a pile of empty paint cans. There are no lids or markings on them, and at first sight they look like horse troughs. They have been carved from solid blocks of granite, and running my finger along one of the chisel marks I think of the dusty mason sweating over his work perhaps a thousand years ago.

After making a silent apology to the previous occupant and assuring him I mean no disrespect, I climb into the largest of the coffins to try and envisage what it must have been like when people were first laid to rest here. It fits me surprisingly well, and I cross my arms on my chest and shut my eyes, hold my breath and listen to the silence. When I worked as a gravedigger in a cemetery in a traffic-ridden part of Portsmouth I was surprised at how silence fell when I was six feet down. It is the same here.

I concentrate till it hurts, trying to summon up a picture of whose last resting place this was. Was it a valiant Templar, laid to rest on his home ground after a lifetime of battling to protect pilgrims to the Holy Land? Had he been wounded or even slain by a Moorish sword, or did he die peacefully in bed, surrounded by a loving family? Or perhaps it was the local butcher or baker who occupied this small space.

Musing on how far away and yet how close the past is, I attempt to rise like Dracula from the coffin, and find I am stuck.

I call for assistance, but my wife has gone off to make friends with a group of hens in a nearby garden.

As I struggle to free myself I hear the sound of many feet scrunching on the gravel path around the chapel.

La Roque-Gageac

I have recovered from the shock and then indignity after being rescued from the coffin by an entire class of adolescent schoolchildren being given a guided tour of the chapel. I told their guardian that I had stepped backwards to get a better view of the gable end of the chapel and tripped over and then fell into the coffin on my back.

We have picked up the trail at another magnificent castle in the sky. La Roque-Gageac is just up the road and river from Domme, and appears to have been created for the sole purpose of selling picture-postcards.

On the north bank of the Dordogne, the huddle of grand and modest dwellings are framed by the backdrop of rugged cliff face, on which sits the remnants of a 12th-century fortress.

Another embellishment is the exotic garden near the church, created in the 1970s and flourishing so well because the plants are protected by the cliff and face the south.

Nearby is the Renaissance Manoir de Tarde, and the whole ensemble is a magnet for tourists, especially those who fancy themselves as photographers. Inching our way along the riverside road, we encounter a heaving knot of people in long shorts, sandals and funny hats. All are waving cameras, some of which must have cost more than our car. The scene reminds me of when I was caught up in a battle between paparazzi struggling to get the best shot of Princess Diana.

But these people are amateurs, and vying to get the best shot of the town. I can see that there is a particularly prime spot, which enables the photographer to capture the most attractive row of houses and the fort while cutting out the mini-convenience store next to the car park. It occurs to me that a shrewd move by the commune would be to rope off the square metre that affords the most photogenic spot, mount a guard and charge visitors a Euro to use it for enough time to reel off a dozen snaps. Across a few seasons, I reckon it would bring in enough revenue to build a discreet underground car park, possibly constructed in medieval style.

Food and Drink

Cheeses In this area include Bleu de Quercy, a soft cow's milk cheese. Chaumes (which literally means 'stubble') also comes from cows and is based upon traditional Trappist cheeses. We find it rubbery, but it is also sold in spreadable form and said to be popular with children.

Once produced in the Allier region but now on farms in the Lot, Truffe du Perigord comes in small, truffle-like black-coated rounds after being 'matured' for a very brief spell in humid cellars.

I don't know what the rate of heart attacks in this area of France is, but we are entering into a place of seriously rich fare.

In particular, you won't go far in the Périgord without bumping into a goose or its constituent parts. We do not usually eat *foie gras* (literally 'fat liver'), mostly because of how it is produced by force-feeding a goose with corn so it goes from six to ten kilos in less than a month. The engorged liver itself can weigh up to a kilo. Another, less sentimental reason we do not buy *foie gras* is because of the outrageous cost.

When the liver has been removed, the meat of the bird is cooked and preserved in its own thick, yellow grease as *confits d'oie*. Another rich delicacy is *cou d'oie farci*, which is goose's neck stuffed with sausage meat, duck liver and truffles. A popular dish from this region is a salad served with warm goose gizzards (*gézier*).

Inevitably, truffles play a big part in Périgord cuisine, and a favourite way of serving them is *à la cendre*, which is wrapped in bacon and cooked in hot ashes.

Fried foie gras with chestnut crumble

If you have no qualms about eating force-fed goose liver, this is an interesting Périgord Noir starter. Or you could go for a much less controversially produced and much less costly type of what we like to call liver paté.

Ingredients

500g foie gras

300g chestnuts

40g non-sugared muesli

70g flour

40g sugar

50g butter

A lettuce

Method

Crush and mix the chestnuts with the muesli, flour, sugar and butter.

Spread the mixture on some baking paper and bake for fifteen minutes.

Fry the foie gras and add some pepper.

Serve with lettuce and walnut oil.

Pommes sarladaises

The French can do (at least) a hundred different interesting things with a potato. This simple way of serving up the common spud is named for Sarlat, but is a dish you will find everywhere in the Périgord.

Ingredients

A kilo of firm potatoes

Three tablespoons of goose or duck fat

Four cloves of garlic

A tablespoon of chopped parsley

Some seasoning

Method

Peel the potatoes, dry thoroughly and cut into slices.

Melt most of the grease in a large heavy pan and sear the potatoes briefly.

Reduce heat and cook for ten minutes, stirring regularly.

When golden all over, add the remaining fat and crushed garlic.

Reduce heat again, cover and let the potatoes sweat for around fifteen minutes, turning occasionally with a wooden spatula. The trick is to get them really soft but not collapsed.

Finally, add parsley and allow the pan to stand for a few moments before serving.

Périgordian Duck Confit

This dish has a lot of variations. In Basque territory there would be mushrooms, in Sarlat it would be served with the *pommes sarladaises* above. In Gascony it would be more of a *pot-au-feu*. The common factor is the duck legs, cooked and preserved in their own fat as a 'confit'.

Ingredients

6-8 confit duck legs

One kg butterbeans

150g smoked lardons

Two onions

Three garlic cloves

Four tomatoes

Three carrots

Sprigs of thyme

Some breadcrumbs

Some seasoning

Method

Soak the beans for several hours (or the day before) and cook in water on a low heat for an hour. Keep the cooking juices.

Peel and thinly slice the onions and garlic.

Take the legs out of the tin and put the fat in a large pan.

Sweat the lardons and onion and garlic, then add the cooked beans and the sliced carrot, chopped tomato and thyme.

Pour in some spoonfuls of the juice from cooking the beans.

Simmer while de-boning the duck legs and adding the meat

to the pan.

Finally, sprinkle with breadcrumbs and brown in the oven.

Périgord Noir Walnut Tart

Walnuts are almost as common as geese and ducks in the Périgord Noir. According to the experts, they've been around in this part of France for at least 17,000 years. At one time, walnut oil was regarded in the same light as gold. November was harvesting time, and the hands of the gatherers were permanently stained. You can still spot a walnut harvester nowadays. This is a really local recipe.

Ingredients

280g all-purpose flour

Two tablespoons sugar

One teaspoon salt

Some cold unsalted butter, cut into small cubes

One large egg

Some iced water

plus:

275 grams fresh walnuts*

160ml double cream

125 ml water

300g sugar

55g unsalted butter

Some salt (optional)

NB. You will need a 9-inch (20-23cm) tart pan with a removable base.

Method

For the dough, whisk together the flour, sugar and salt.

Blend in the butter till the mix is coarsely 'crumby' with some pea-sized lumps of butter remaining.

Beat together the egg with three tablespoons of iced water and stir in the flour mix.

Test by squeezing a small handful together. If it does not hold, add a little more ice water. Do not overwork.

Make the mix into a 5-inch (13cm) disk, wrap in film and chill for an hour.

Roll out the dough between two sheets of plastic film to a 12-inch (30cm) round and fit into your tart pan (after discarding the film!) with the dough protruding slightly above the edge of the pan.

Preheat oven to 425F/218°C.

Now line a baking tray with foil and lightly toast the walnuts for five minutes.

Transfer the walnuts to a bowl.

Heat the cream in a small pan over a low heat.

Boil the water and sugar till the sugar has dissolved, ensuring all grains are washed from sides of pan.

Continue to boil without stirring but occasionally swirling until caramel colours to an even amber.

Remove from heat and slowly add cream, which will bubble furiously.

When the bubbling subsides, add walnuts and butter and cook over a medium heat for a couple of minutes, stirring now and then.

Pour the filling into the pastry-lined tart pan and sprinkle with sugar.

Bake for 25 minutes, checking regularly and covering with foil if top is becoming too brown in spots.

Reduce oven to 325F/160°C and bake for around fifteen minutes until filling is set and crust is golden.

Cool and remove from pan.

NB: *If you're a purist and bought your walnuts in shell, you may like to know that it is said that the people of Sarlat crush the shells and use them as kitty litter.*

Drink

Although some thirty different wines are produced in the Périgord Noir, they are mostly of the Vin de Pays grade, and produced from muscadelle, chardonnay, sauvignon blanc, merlot and malbec grapes.

Vin de Pays ('country wine') is or was a qualification which was above table wines but below AOC, of which we have talked previously. Unlike table wines, of which the only requirement is that it comes from France, Vin de Pays has a geographic designation, and wines bearing that stamp can only be made from certain varieties or blends.

In 2009, The Vin de Pays appellation was replaced by the designation IGP (*Indication Géographique Protégé* or Protected Geographic Region). The country concerned being France, most of the growers have not bothered to make the change of nomenclature.

Once upon a time, this part of Périgord was awash with vineyards; nowadays they are very thin on the ground. There is the Domme Vineyard which is open to visitors all year round, and is to be found a few miles south of the town for which it is named.

LEG 5

Castelnaud-la-Chapelle to Bergerac

Distance: 65 kilometres

Region: Aquitaine

Department: The Dordogne

Castelnaud-la-Chapelle

It's not often you see castles having a staring-out contest.

The village of Castelnaud-la-Chapelle sits inoffensively alongside the river. Above it looms a truly forbidding castle, apparently put there to confront its rival at nearby Beynac.

Records date the castle to the 13th century, and it has a more-than-usually bloody history. Nowadays it's in private hands, but open to the public. Inside its walls you can see how these great fortresses defended themselves, and how they were brought down. There is an interesting museum of medieval warfare, which features reproductions of a variety of siege engines and other machines for dealing death and destruction. In season there are exhibitions of how the giant slingshot trebuchet was operated, but unlike other demonstrations of ancient machinery I doubt tourists are allowed to try their hands.

Nearby and at a lower level is the much more modest Château Milandes, which was a comfy alternative for the owners of the fortress when they were not under siege. In more recent times it was owned by the legendary American-born French singer and dancer Josephine Baker.

It is a long hike up to the main fortress from the free car park, so we pay for a space much closer, though I resent handing over three Euros to a surly individual guarding the entrance. Especially as he is wearing no uniform and offers no tickets. He also offered me no change from a five Euro note until I reminded him. This reminds me of a probably apocryphal tale about a Norman friend of a friend who claimed to make a good living in the summer months by standing at the gates of free car parks and looking official with his hand out.

After doing the castle we stop off at the nearby Nut Museum. It may not sound like a must-visit venue, but we found it well worth the trouble on account of the conversation-stopping facts available. For instance, how many people know that Louis XI's beard was trimmed with hot walnut shells, and walnuts were used in the insulation of American spacecraft?

Beynac-et-Cazenac

Although on the other side of the river, Castlenaud's great rival is almost with spitting distance.

Though Beynac-et-Cazenac gets the earliest mention in 12th-century records, both castles and the villages they supported share commonalities. At a little over 500, the population of both are about the same. Both castles were at some time in the hands of one of the Simons de Montfort, and both are in permanent running for the title of Most Beautiful Village in France. The castle at Beynac has the additional distinction of being occupied by Richard the Lionheart in 1189. During the Hundred Years War, the French castle of Castelnaud and the English castle of Beynac glared at each other across the river and engaged in a number of inconclusive confrontations.

I feel I know Beynac-et-Cazenac before we get there, as I have been virtually visiting it in the company of a Victorian wayfarer. Edward Harrison Barker is that rarest of travel writers, whose style makes it seem he is chatting to you in a bar or over dinner. This easy-readability is even more remarkable when you consider that he was writing at a time when a casual style and informal use of language was hardly the norm.

Though I could not find out much about him, it is known that Barker spent fifteen years towards the end of the 19th century wandering around France, often in the Aquitaine region. His account of taking a house in Beynac for a summer's lease makes engaging reading, but he is not one of those upper-class Victorians who painted chocolate-box and bucolic word pictures of the people and places they encountered. As well as describing everyday life in Beynac with humour and warmth, he does not shrink from what life was like for real people. A fine example is his conversations with Old Suzette, a fisherman's widow who could be of any age between 50 and 70. He describes taking a photograph of her and how, on seeing it, she put her head in her apron and wept. She had not known, she told him, that she had grown so old and ugly.

But, this remarkable woman was grateful for what Providence had brought her. She had a tiny cottage and kitchen garden, with fruit in the summer and walnuts and chestnuts for the winter. In good times, there would be a piece of fat bacon hanging from a beam in the kitchen, and a sliver would add flavour to the water thickened with bread and beans which she called soup. At one of their meetings, Suzette told of how, when her husband was alive, she would walk the eight miles to Sarlat market to sell his catch. So as not to miss the early customers she would leave at two in the morning and travel the uphill route through dark woods where bad people lurked and wolves often howled. In winter, she would arrive so numb with the cold that she would not be able to take the basket of fish from her head unaided.

As we and other sleek tourists wander around 'folk' museums and envisage what appears to have been an idyllic rural age, it is instructive to learn about and consider what life was really like for most people in the not-so-distant past.

St-Cyprien

It is that time of day when my wife and I may fall out over accommodation plans.

In essence, she wants to stop at the first campsite or hotel we encounter as dusk approaches. I invariably want to press on until we find a better place to stay. How I can tell that the places we pass are below par compared with what is to come is a question I find difficult to answer. But today has been exceptionally hot and sticky and I am too tired to protest when she points out the sign for a camp site on the river banks directly below our next place of call. In accord, we navigate a hump-back bridge and follow the directions.

At the gate, the poster claims that Le Camping du Garrit occupies a little corner of Paradise, nestling in a valley of castles, historic sites and classic gastronomy. So far so good.

Arriving at the cottage serving as a reception area, first impressions are that we have happened upon a promising site. It is small, privately owned and in a secluded position directly on the river, and there is a swimming pool with no users. It also looks uncrowded, as the owner of a pizza van sits glumly at the wheel, watching the smoke from his wood-fired oven spiral up into the still evening air.

The reception area is the front room of small cottage which is obviously home to the owners, and they are clearly pleased to see us. Although it is late June and this part of France is in the grip of a heatwave, the season has not begun so the site is far from busy. The small, elderly man at the desk is my sort of campsite owner, as, when I ask where we should pitch our tent, he makes an expansive gesture and invites us to help ourselves. When I ask at what time the barrier comes down and between what hours the pool is open, he looks at me rather strangely. The barrier will stay up to suit us, and the pool-like the bar-is open all the time there is a customer. When I ask him for any other rules, he thinks a bit, does a mild shrug and says he cannot think of any, then asks if I could manage a cold beer.

*   *   *

My wife has worked her magic with the tent, we have had a swim and a shower and are now investigating the fleshpots of St. Cyprien.

The town is named for a hermit who set up home in a cave overlooking the Dordogne Valley in 620 AD. Somewhat contrary to the general job-description of a hermit, he sought out company and eventually established a thriving monastic community.

Unlike many of the picture-postcard villages and towns on the tourist route, St Cyprien is a place of two very definite halves. The remains of the monastery and old town are at the top of the hill, awash with winding, cobbled street, bits of impressive rampart, well-preserved and characterful old houses and posh-ish restaurants.

Below the old town and surrounding the through road are all the practical requirements of a modern community. We are glad to find an air-conditioned bar on the outskirts, where two pretty barmaids are watching a group of cool young men playing pool. After ordering our drinks, I asked if anyone knew where we could get something to eat in town.

In Britain, I would have been ignored or told where the nearest takeaway was.

Here, the game was put on hold and the players went into consultation with the bar staff to compare notes and come up with recommendations. One of the poolists nominated a fish restaurant, but was outvoted by two others who said their standards had been slipping. One of the barmaids said there was a traditional French restaurant with a very reasonable all-inclusive menu of 50 Euros a head, but her friend said it was fully booked every night. Perhaps, the only other occupant of the bar suggested, we might enjoy a visit to the *Marché Gourmande*?

We arrive in the square at the top of the town to find I have literally misinterpreted the helpful customer at the bar.

(153)

The evening event is not a market for gourmets, but for gluttons.

Long rows of trestle tables and benches take up the centre ground, and are ringed with a dozen stalls, each vying to give off the most delicious aroma. The French are normally hyper-critical of food from other cultures, unless, as with pizza and pasta, they consider it no threat to their supremacy. But this evening's gathering is a celebration of international cuisine. Apart from the duck confit and chips, there are stalls serving Vietnamese, Dutch, German and, astonishingly, English specialities. Admittedly the English stall offering is restricted to fish and chips, which is about the only British meal the French think edible, but it is still a remarkable sight.

We have joined the queue at the Vietnamese stall, and it is interesting to note who is patronising which types of cuisine. The two French-themed stalls are predictably under siege, mostly by older people. The youngsters are mostly going for the pizza stand. There is a fair queue for the fish and chips, but all the people waiting are locals. Nearly all those waiting in line for Chinese and Vietnamese are holidaying or holiday home-owning Brits.

One can easily distinguish between the two as the holidaymakers conduct themselves respectfully and as if they are grateful for being allowed to join in the event. The Brits with homes in or around St Cyprien mostly act as if they own the town, which in little bits I suppose they do. As in Domme, the air is filled with the braying calls of the English middle classes, discussing the latest gossip or the problems they are having with their wayward *fosse septique*.

My wife and I share the intimate secrets of at least a dozen people we do not know, then their prattle is drowned out as the DJ goes into action.

It is generally accepted that French pop music is the worst in Europe, even including Italy and Moldova. Not so well-known is that France is home to easily the worst disc jockeys in the world. All speak quickly and largely unintelligibly. Coming from one of the fastest-speaking nations in the world, French DJs are naturally streets ahead when it comes to the words per second count. They also speak in a monotone, with no cadence, pause or pitch changes to alleviate the machine-gun delivery. The one on duty at St Cyprien was also getting on a bit and had obviously had a few bracing drinks before turning on the microphone. Oddly, his overall appearance and presentational techniques added to rather than detracted from our evening. The man in the white suit, comb-over haircut and Cuban heels acted as a sort of Pied Piper by drawing all the children to the far end of the square. We were left to enjoy what, because of the seating arrangements, seemed like a giant dinner party with guests eating different things and talking different languages.

By one in the morning, our greed was finally assuaged and we were sitting on the ramparts, finishing off a bottle of exceptionally pleasant Merlot. We had started out arguing about the constellations and what and where they were, but agreed to disagree as it would have been a shame to spoil such a perfect night.

Urval

A glorious Sunday morning and everyone seems intent on making the most of the day.

Kayaks, shiny new canoes, battered, flat bottomed metal fishing boats and the odd windsurfer jostle on the water; cars and campers harry and shepherd their fellow travellers beside the river in an endless stream. The roadside is dotted with stalls selling local fruit, seasonal vegetables, flowers, mushrooms, souvenirs and even painfully expensive truffles.

Between the river and road, people work or wander in vineyards, tobacco fields and through hosts of swaying sunflowers and serried ranks of walnut trees. Above all this activity, unconcerned buzzards circle lazily and spread their wings to accept the warmth of the morning sun.

Tired of being bullied by a red-faced man with a stupid face to match his hat who is driving a huge camper he thinks is a sports car, we escape the river of traffic by turning off at a sign promising a communal oven and 12th-century church. The contrast between there and here is almost spine-tingling.

Urval would be many people's idea of an ideal place to spend one's declining years. It is close but out of sound of the nearest main road and lies at the bottom of what is almost a dead-end.

Editors of glossy magazines would slather after photographs of the ancient but beautifully preserved and restored Périgordian cottages dotted along a peaceful stream winding its way through a meadow to the sluice gate and picture-postcard mill.

Overseeing this almost painfully seductive scene is a church which reeks of history, and alongside it a giant oven once shared by the commune. Nearby is the equally picturesque accommodation for the *fournier*, whose job it was to look after the oven, and next to that what is said to be the original *pigeonnier*. A plaque tells us that the oven-master's wages would be paid by the local landlord (*seigneur*) from the fees he received from the villagers for the use of the giant bread oven.

We picnic by the stream and share our baguette with the swans, who disdainfully ignore my very British chocolate digestive biscuits. A little distance away stands the 15th-century Château de la Bourlie, the gardens of which are advertised as Most Notable. I do not know if this is true, but this oasis of calm is certainly a most notable place. It is not till we say goodbye to the swans and drive away that we realise that they are the only living beings we have seen for the past hour. My wife proposes that Urval is actually a full size model village with no inhabitants, but I think the villagers just know when they are on to a good thing and do not want to encourage visitors by talking to them.

*   *   *

We continue on the road, unconcerned about the likely presence of Gendarmes lying in wait. Sunday is a happy hunting day for *Les Flic*, and a favourite trick is to mount a highly visible presence on a roundabout or intersection. Passing at a crawl, gullible motorists will then speed away and be caught by a posse round the next corner.

We are not worried about speeding as the weight of traffic makes us all responsible drivers, and in any case it is not long after noon. The cops will be at lunch but out in force later to spoil someone's day with a hefty fine. If the drivers they stop are over the limit the penalty could be more serious.

The French operate a graduated system of bans based on the level of alcohol in the blood of the offender. A lengthy ban can be a real problem for people living in isolated places, but in a very French way they can always buy one of the tiny cars which do not require a licence. Some people say that they were created for drunk drivers, and it would be interesting to find out what happens if a previously banned driver were to fail a breath test while driving one. Would he be above the law and free to go on his way, or have to buy another licence-free machine?

A telling statistic emerged after a survey in 2007. It found that Britain has less than 5000 licence-free cars on its roads. Spain had 6000, Italy 49,000...and France a massive 140,000.

France has a particularly bad record on accidents and injuries caused by drink-driving, and in 2012 the Government announced a scheme to reduce the carnage. From July of that year, it would become law for all motor vehicles to carry two breathalysers for self-testing. There would be a fine for those transgressing the law.

In October of the same year it was announced that the fine for not carrying the breathalysers was to be 'postponed'. By then, of course, millions of French and foreign drivers and riders had invested in the kit, bringing in lots and lots of tax money.

By January of the next year, the Government announced that the fine had been put on hold indefinitely'. So in theory it is still a legal requirement to carry two breathalysers when you are on the road, but there will be no punishment if you don't.

Limeuil and Trémolat

The views are still luscious and we are in danger of panorama fatigue. I have often thought how curious it is that visitors pay a lot of money to go and wonder at spectacular natural and man-made features, but the people who live there seem to take them for granted. After our non-stop feasting on spectacular features and castles, I can see how that could happen.

As it is our duty to give both fair coverage, we take successive coffees at the picturesque villages of Limeuil and Trémolat and find they have the same sort of duality we found at Beynac and Castlenaud.

Both are situated on oxbow bends in the river, have around the same headcount and even vie for the ongoing Best View of the Dordogne title.

With an acute accent on the 'e', *cinglé* means mad, loopy or round the bend. Without the accent it becomes an extreme description of a bend in a river. We visited the viewpoints at Limeuil and Trémolat and thought there was not a lot to choose between them.

Nowadays, both villages have a relaxed, friendly and almost 'arty' feel, but it was not always so. At various times in their long history they have paid unwilling host to marauding Vikings and English soldiery, and now are quite pleased to welcome foreign tourists and their money. Trémolat also has a claim to fame for being the setting for the macabre 1970s thriller, *Le Boucher*.

Eymet

We are on route to Bergerac but cannot by-pass the chance to drop in on a town which is famous countrywide for the number of its expatriate and second-home- owning Britons.

When the bastide town of Eymet was founded in 1270 by the brother of Louis IX, I bet he had no idea it would become an English enclave. Nor that there would be a television documentary series made about the Brits living there.

I can understand how places like Birmingham attracted many Asian settlers, and why Boston is a magnet for so many Poles. People moving to live in a country which does not speak their language often like to stick together and create a familiar culture on foreign soil. What makes Eymet a curiosity for me is that nearly all Britons I know who have moved to live in France have done their best to avoid having even a single English neighbour. Or at least that is what they claimed. In Spain of course, British expats do their best to re-create home surroundings. As anyone who has watched a half-naked Brit sweating bucket loads while fighting his way through a full Sunday roast dinner on the seafront at Torremolinos will know, we like to stick to our old ways and kind wherever in the world we are.

But not so-allegedly-in France. I have consistently found that many Brits who move to live in France will go to great lengths (sometimes literally) to distance themselves from other fellow-countrymen and women who are doing exactly the same. It is quite common to see this type of expat pretending to be French when finding themselves in the same supermarket queue as holidaying Brits.

But not so in Eymet. Totally against the declared attitude of so many other expats, the 10,000 British residents of Eymet have, according to many sources done their best to turn their corner of a foreign field into a Little England. The cricket team recently celebrated its 25th birthday, one of the elected officials is a Briton, and there is a traditional corner shop selling British pork sausages and Marmite.

There is always criticism about the idea of British expats gathering together in a foreign country. But I can't see what all the fuss is about. The same sort of snotty middle-class Brit critics would not, of course, complain about immigrants taking over communities in Britain, but that is typical of the woolly thinking of your classic Guardianista English *bien pensant*.

Bergerac

To some, the word 'Bergerac' would conjure up a very passable wine. Others would think of a fictional character with an enormous nose. Some would even recall a fictional 1970s television series about a Jersey-based private investigator. It is a thought-provoking fact that that if you Google the word, *Bergerac*, the long-dead TV series occupies three of the top five spots in the listings.

We are heading for one of our favourite French towns, and by so doing have passed into Purple Périgord territory. As discussed earlier, the name reflects the colour of most of the vast acreage of grapes grown here.

Bergerac gets its name from an 11th-century castle built on a bank of the Dordogne, and round which a town quickly grew. It was on the route of pilgrims heading for Spain and Santiago de Compostela, and also became an important staging post for trading between Bordeaux and the interior. The wine trade played an increasingly important part in the town's economy from the Middle Ages. It was a Protestant stronghold in the sixteenth century and became known as the Geneva of France. But Bergerac's prosperity was based upon the wine and tobacco trade, and it is said the town's fountains ran red when Louis XIII stopped by in 1621.

Nowadays, the wine trade is one of the biggest in the region, and Bergerac is the commercial capital for the tobacco trade for the whole of the country. Perhaps it is its long devotion to human pleasures and indulgences that lends the town the easy-going air we have observed on a dozen visits.

The most famous son of the town is, of course, Cyrano de Bergerac and we never visit without paying our respects to the life-sized statue with a truly monstrous hooter which stands in the Place de Cayla.

Ironically, there is no real connection between the town and the legendary swordsman whose love life was ruined by his oversized nose.

Hercule-Savinien Cyrano de Bergerac was born near Paris in 1619. Not many people know that he was one of the earliest pioneers of the science-fiction genre, and in *Voyage dans la Lune* in 1657 he travels to the moon with the propulsive aid of fire crackers.

As to the true size of his proboscis, contemporary portraits do indeed show him with an unusually large nose, and some biographers claim he fought more than a thousand duels because of it. Others say he was gay. It does appear that he devoted much of his adult life to gambling, drinking and fighting. The cause of his premature end at the age of 36 is just as contentious. One camp claims he died in a street fight, the other that he was simply hit by a falling plank.

The Cyrano we all know was actually the creation of Parisian poet Edmond Rostand, and his comedy drama *Cyrano de Bergerac* was an immediate and unexpected hit when it was staged in the capital in 1897. It ran for 300 consecutive nights, and the legend of the swashbuckling tragic hero was born.

Another thing I like about Bergerac is that it is one of those not-so-common places where young and old rub shoulders without a trace of friction. We took lunch in the old town, and it was aswarm with students gathering at ultra-modern and modish bars and oldies pottering around to look at the ancient building.

In most places the mix would not have worked. Here it seemed that old and new could live in perfect harmony.

Food & Drink

Unsurprisingly, menus and tables here are crowded with dishes composed mostly of goose and duck and associated products. They even manage to get duck fat into their bread, as you will see below. Let's start our Périgordian meal with a choice of two simple soups:

Soupe à la l'ail

Ingredients

One bulb of garlic

One egg

One litre of water

One spoonful of duck fat

A tablespoon of flour

A drizzle of vinegar

Method

Peel the cloves and fry in the duck fat till golden brown.

Quickly add the flour, mix well and then add the water.

Bring to the boil.

Separate the egg, add a few drops of vinegar to the yolk, then add to the water while stirring to prevent coagulation.

Still stirring, add the egg white and season.

The soup is traditionally served poured over stale bread.

Soupe aux Oignons

Ingredients

250g onions

A clove of garlic

A litre of chicken stock

Three tablespoons tomato purée

Two egg yolks

Some goose fat

One tablespoon flour

Some bread

Salt and pepper

Method

Peel and finely chop the onions and fry in the goose fat.

Sprinkle with flour and cover with the chicken stock.

Add the peeled, crushed garlic and the tomato purée.

Season to taste and leave to cook for half an hour.

Meanwhile, toast some thin slices of country bread and put in soup bowls and then pepper.

Mix the egg yolks in a little stock then pour into the soup, stirring all the while and not allowing to boil.

Pour the soup over the bread and serve.

Duck foie gras and peach pie with caramel and sea salt sauce

Ingredients

Two peaches

320g fresh duck foie gras

Four individual discs of flaky pastry

50g butter

Some additional flaky pastry

150g granulated sugar

Quarter of a litre single cream

10g coarse sea salt

Some water

Method

Place the sliced peaches in a pan and fry in butter.

Put aside but keep warm.

Slice the foie gras and pan-fry.

Season and set aside.

Place the rounds of pastry in shallow pie dishes and cook in oven at 200°C for ten minutes or so.

Fill the pies with the peaches and foie gras.

Cut the remaining pastry into strips and arrange in lattice style over the filling.

Cook in oven for five minutes.

For the sauce, heat the sugar in a little water till it forms a golden syrupy caramel, then add the salt and cream.

Perigordian walnut molten cakes

A sacristan can be either a person in charge of a sacristy in the Catholic Church, or the sexton of a parish church. They may also be little twisted twiglets of pastry, as in this very traditional Black Périgordian recipe.

Ingredients

125g softened butter

150g flour

100g sugar

Three eggs

50g finely chopped walnuts

5g baking powder

Some walnut liqueur (if you can get it)

Some whipping cream

Some flaky pastry

(You will also need a tray of small cake moulds)

Method

Butter the moulds and sprinkle with a little sugar, then shake out the excess (this helps prevent sticking).

Whisk together the rest of the sugar and the eggs in a bowl, then blend in the flour, baking powder, softened butter and walnuts.

Put the mixture in the moulds and bake in an oven at 180°C for ten minutes.

For the walnut liqueur cream, whip the cream with some sugar and add liqueur. If you can't find any walnut liqueur, improvise and just use the cream and sugar.

For the sacristans, roll out the flaky pastry and cut into

strips.

Roll in the granulated sugar and walnut pieces.

Twist the strips and bake in an oven at 180°C till lightly browned.

Serve with walnut ice cream (again, improvise if you need).

La Mique

This Périgordian favourite is a cross between a bread and a dumpling, and is traditionally poached in a stew or juice from pork or other meat. When cooked, leftovers may be eaten with jam or other sweet spread for breakfast.

Ingredients

500g flour

Two eggs

80g melted goose fat

25cl milk

20g yeast

Salt

Method

Warm the milk and mix in the yeast.

Add the flour, salt and goose fat and break the eggs into the centre of the mix.

Mix until firm and doughy, then dust with flour, wrap in a cloth and leave to rise for two hours. The resulting 'mique' can be served in place of bread, or with stews and meat sauces, or with vegetables, salted pork and chitterling sausages.

Drink

This is of course very serious wine country. The vineyards surrounding Bergerac on both sides of the river cover 13,000 hectares (over 32,000 acres) on 93 villages. There are 13 'Appellations' some of the most familiar of which are AOC Bergerac (red, white, dry and rosé), Cotes de Bergerac (red and semi-sweet white wine), Pércharmant (red) and Rosette (semi-sweet white).

Monbazillac is a village on the left bank of the Dordogne, opposite Bergerac. It is surrounded by around 5000 acres of vineyards, and is famed for its sweet white wine. It has only held an AOC designation since 1936, but the area has a long history of producing classy sweet white wines. A good example is Saussignac.

Also found here is Montravel (red, dry white and semi-sweet white). The blend and choice of Cabernet Sauvignon, Cabernet France, Merlot, Malbec for the reds and Sauvignon, Sémillon, Muscadelle for the whites determines the characteristic flavours of Bergerac wines.

LEG 6

Bergerac to Blaye

Distance: 124 kilometres

Region: Aquitaine

Departments: The Dordogne, The Gironde

After a wistful visit to the National Tobacco Museum, we leave Bergerac and head westward towards a new department. It transpires we are also heading into contentious waters.

The riverside town of Gardonne is around 40km downstream of Bergerac. Paddle your canoe along the south side of the river and you will be in the Dordogne department. Cross to the north bank and you will find yourself in the department of the Gironde.

What concerns us is what the river should be called from this point until it empties into the sea via the biggest estuary in France.

Arguments have long raged and people become quite exercised about the subject. Basically, one side says that the river is now in the Gironde department, and more of the water in it comes from the river of that name. Logic thus dictates that it should be known as the Gironde River. Dordognians say the river should keep its given name until it meets with a liquid readily identifiable as seawater. Diplomatically and I suspect not wishing to take sides and alienate one camp, most mapmakers show both names.

From our perspective, there is a village called Pessac-sur-Dordogne 30 kilometres on from Gardonne, and one assumes the people who named it and lived there know what they were talking about. Besides, it would seem wimpish to end our journey at some wishy-washy and undetermined point.

We decide to be scrupulously fair in this matter, and stop and ask ten passing locals the name of the river. Nine said it was the Dordogne, and one said it was the Loire. He had obviously just had a very good lunch, so could be forgiven his lack of geographical awareness.

Ste-Foy-La-Grande

Judging by our brief visit, this is a very trendy place. Dozens of restaurants line the grid of streets alongside the river, and all seem busy. It is one of the smallest communes in France, occupying only five hectares, which may be why it seems a permanently busy and buzzy place.

The quality of the cars lining the streets suggests that there is no shortage of disposable income in this area. Bordeaux is only an hour away, and St Émilion is just 30k to the north. I have heard the town described as a place of faded French beauty, and if pushed for an anthropomorphic comparison, I could indeed and at a push see Ste-Foy-La-Grande as Catherine Deneuve.

The town also makes it to the top hundred rankings out of what must be the tens of thousands of farmers' markets in France, though I do not know who does the judging.

'Foy' or 'Fides' is the French equivalent of Faith, and the town gets its name from a martyr who died in 1298 at the hands of one of the madder Roman Emperors.

Gaul was in the possession of Maximian, who thought of himself as a god and did not approve of Christians. A group of soldiers decided to make an example of someone in the area and a young girl was stripped, tied to a griddle and roasted over a bonfire. An angel intervened and sent down a cloud to cover her nakedness, which I am sure was a great consolation to the roasted virgin.

After looking round the town we do some window shopping and decide to visit the local Super U for the makings of a picnic on the river bank. We buy some burgers but I do not get our portable griddle out as it would seem insensitive given our location.

Saint-Michel-de-Montaigne

In general, the French tend to treat their philosophers more like rock gods or film stars than people who can think a bit, and the deader they are, the more revered.

Michel de Montaigne was a key figure of the French Renaissance, and his essays had a direct influence on such eminent thinkers like René Descartes, Ralph Waldo Emerson and William Hazlitt, to say nothing of Isaac Asimov and William Shakespeare.

Montaigne was born in 1533 in the town just north of the Dordogne which is now named for him or perhaps his family. He was born into enormous wealth and privilege, and though the family home no longer exists, the tower in which he did most of his thinking and writing still stands.

If ever a boy was groomed for stardom it was Montaigne. His father was so intent on ensuring a classic education for his son that only Latin was spoken in his presence in his early years. A musician would wake him each morning, and intellectual discussions would take place in Ancient Greek.

In 1571, Montaigne retreated from public life and took to his tower, locking himself in with at least 15,000 books. The great man died of quinsy* at the age of 59, leaving behind a large number of essays, the aim of which was to describe his fellow beings with utter frankness.

I have not read much of his writings and it wasn't his fault he was born to immense wealth and privilege, but it seems to me he had a pretty enviable life. Much of which was spent looking down from his tower on the peasantry slogging away in his family's fields as he pondered on how they and their lives could best be arranged.

*In case you didn't know (as I didn't), quinsy is a severe inflammation of the throat near a tonsil, and which can lead to an abscess.

Castillon-la-Bataille

Nearing the end of the river and our journey, we arrive at the place where more than a century of brutal warfare in this region came to a climactic finale.

The Hundred Years war actually lasted more than a hundred years, and officially began in 1337. It had its roots in the Norman Conquest, but was essentially a titanic battle for control of huge swathes of France between England's House of Plantagenet and France's House of Valois.

In 1452, John Talbot, Earl of Shrewsbury was summoned by the English king Edward IV and ordered to lead an army to relieve Bordeaux, which had been taken by the French in the previous year. Talbot was a very, very old man at and for the time, and some say well into his eighties. But he was chosen because he was held in great stead by English troops and the influential citizens of the major occupied cities.

Perhaps curiously and certainly unlike in other occupied territories (e.g. Ireland, and Scotland), the English occupiers in this region treated the French justly and were wise enough to give them some form of autonomy. The wisdom of this enlightened approach was demonstrated when Talbot arrived with 4000 men and Bordeaux rose against its French masters and threw wide the town gates.

A French army was immediately despatched to re-take Bordeaux, and their commander decided that Castillon was the best place to confront the English troops. Accordingly, their leader the unheroically named Jean Bureau drew up his forces on the bank of the Dordogne just east of the town, and set about setting up earthworks and wooden ramparts made from tree trunks.

Meanwhile, Talbot was on the move, his force now swollen to 6000 men. Laying in wait was Bureau's main body, and a force of 800 archers who were grouped around an ancient abbey at the foot of a wooded hill to the north of Castillon.

Talbot was expected to approach the enemy along the broad valley, which was heavily cultivated and offered no cover. Instead, he led his troops through a wooded area at the top of the hill and descended on the unprepared archers, slaughtering them to a man.

Deciding to rest his troops, Talbot set up camp at the abbey and allowed them to toast their success with the contents of the cellar.

The momentous day of July 17th, 1453 broke, and one of the last of the Mediaeval Crusader knights prepared for a great victory. Clad in iron and mounted on a white horse, the elderly warrior led a thousand knights and their esquires in a charge against the enemy redoubt. Intelligence had led Talbot to believe that the French were in disarray. In fact, they were waiting with three hundred *bombardes* - an early form of cannon, which fired stone balls.

The missiles wreaked havoc upon horses and riders, and the ground was quickly carpeted with heavily armoured men. They were as helpless, as it was said, as turned turtles, and those who were not fatally wounded by the shot were ridden over by their comrades.

Attacking the ramparts, Talbot's infantry feared no better. The fact was that they were essentially a mediaeval army, fighting with ancient tactics against modern weapons of war.

The attacked now became the attackers, and Talbot led his remaining troops heroically into the fray. Contemporary reports say that he struck out at his comrades when they tried to persuade him to fall back from the inevitable defeat, and it was said that it was as if he preferred to die than live with the memory of failure.

The battle became ever more ferocious, and Talbot and his son were slaughtered along with a huge swathe of English nobility.

Castillon immediately surrendered, and the French king led the siege of Bordeaux in person. When that town fell, the others succumbed, and the whole province was returned to the sceptre and crown of France. As one chronicler put it, after three hundred years in the claws of the English leopard, Guyenne was once again truly French.

Some accounts say Talbot was buried where he fell, cut down by a stone fired from the death-dealing cause of his defeat and the symbol of a complete change to warfare. Wherever he fell or was buried, all that remains on the site now are two simple memorials. One marks the death of the last great English Crusader; the other the termination of the Hundred Years War.

We leave the ancient battlefield in reflective mood, and wonder - perhaps irreverently - if the deluge of English bloodshed in the long war is part of the reason we Brits find this part of France so appealing... and so somehow familiar.

Libourne

Of all the major towns along the river, we find Libourne the least appealing. Because of their elevated and defended locations, many other *bastide* towns have resisted the siege of modernity. But Libourne is now ringed and riven by tacky commercial premises which destroy any sense of the past you get when approaching other ancient towns. Garages, supermarkets and Planet Cash stores shout for attention, and there is a general air of depressed unenthusiasm when we finally reach the town centre.

As we park, unhappy-looking people lounge in doorways, sucking on cigarettes and regarding us and other visitors incuriously. For no logical reason, Libourne reminds us of a mining town in the north of England where the pit has long closed and no new industry has emerged. It says something that an internet list of the top six must-see things in the town is topped by a statue of an army captain who was killed in a colonial battle in1845.

Ironically, Libourne was once the premier port of the Dordogne river. It was here that the great flat-bottomed *gabares* would arrive at the end of their one-way journey to discharge their cargos before suffering the indignity of being turned into firewood. British freighters would beat up the estuary to load with wines from St Émilion, Pomerol and Fronsac. Then, ships got bigger and roads better and the river traffic trade went into decline. There are some fine 18th-century houses with impressive wrought iron balconies overlooking the square to remind the modern visitor of the town's significant past, but we found it rather a gloomy place.

Libourne's main claim to fame now seems to be that it stages the largest fresh food market in the region every week, and that it is twinned with Keynsham. That's K.E.Y.N.S.H.A.M.*

* This reference will only make sense to anyone old enough

to have spent their formative years listening to the ebb and flow of Radio Luxembourg, the only source of pop music on the airwaves in the 1950s.If you are agog to be in on a wrinkly item of nostalgia, just Google 'Horace Batchelor' and all will be revealed.

Bordeaux

Everywhere the vine holds sway, and we begin to panic as the magnetic influence of Bordeaux takes hold.

Though we have travelled the equivalent of to the moon and back on French roads, we still fall prey to the way very big French towns do their best, like black holes, to suck any passing traffic into their maws.

Being the biggest, Paris is naturally the worst. On our first visit by car I became trapped like a fly on the web that is the Boulevard Périphérique, and basically the busiest dual-carriageway in Europe. Considering the standards of French and particularly Parisian driving and the lack of sensible (or sometimes any) signage, I really thought we might be doomed to spend the rest of our lives orbiting the capital. Before we escaped, my wife quite seriously asked me if there was more than one Eiffel Tower in the town, and the experience left its scars. This is basically why we never visit the bigger French towns, and Bordeaux is sixth on the list, size-wise.

After three false starts and sighting the same closed-down *auberge* five times, we manage to escape and head away from Bordeaux on a route not shown on our atlas. My wife says it is because I insist on using the ten year old Michelin and there have been some changes since it was first printed, but I still think it is part of a conspiracy to deceive and distract foreign visitors.

Just for the record and in case you are feeling braver than we, Bordeaux is the 'capital' of this region, and is indeed known to its admirers as the Pearl of Aquitaine.

Another nickname is 'Sleeping Beauty', apparently because of the once pollution -blackened walls of its centre.

Unsurprisingly when you see the extent of the surrounding vineyards, the town is acknowledged as the premier wine industry centre in the world, and certainly stages the planet's biggest yearly wine fair. Bordeaux wine has been produced since the 8th century, and the annual trade in the metropolitan areas is worth, wait for it, 14.5 *billion* Euros. Apart from fear influencing our decision not to visit, Bordeaux does not technically come under our remit as it was built and remains on the banks of the Garonne. But it is only a few miles from our river and has contributed greatly to the success of the Dordogne as a watery commercial highway.

We have decided to mark the end of our latest small adventure by doing something we have not done in 30 years of travelling in France.

In August 1999, Gironde-born farmer José Bové became a national hero. He earned the admiration of millions of French people by dismantling a branch of McDonald's which was under construction in his local town in the Avyron. This direct action meant he was immediately and inevitably hailed throughout the media as a simple farmer standing up to the imperialistic designs and ambitions of an American company intent on filling the stomachs of French children with junk food.

In fact, Bové was a one-time anarchist and political activist and had long been a member of hard-line agricultural unions. The attack on McDonald's was not about the threat to traditional French food values, but a protest about the USA ban on the importation of Roquefort cheese, of which he was a producer. After a hugely drawn out legal battle, he was sentenced in 2002 to three months imprisonment, of which he served 44 days.

Bové went on to write several books and actually stood for President in the election of 2007. In 2009, he became a representative of the South-West in the European Parliament so did very well out of the McDonald's attack. The incident and movement against the fast food chain did not seem to hinder their colonising progress, however, and there are now more than 1300 outlets nationwide.

It is said by foodies that McDonald's outlets in France do not seem like McDonald's outlets elsewhere. In a Paris McDo (as they like to call them) you can get croissants and café crème instead of a Raspberry and White Chocolate Muffin and a Smarties McFlurry. There is even a McBaguette, which seems almost a contradiction in terms. Ironically after all the protests, France is the second biggest consumer of Big Macs outside the United States.

A final irony and a sign of changing times came in 2014 with a noisy protest about the construction of a McDonald's in a small town near Lille. This time rather than trying to stop the branch opening, the protestors were demonstrating because the local council had put a stop to the works because of non-conformation with building regulations.

*   *   *

Our first visit to a McDonald's outlet has been an almost surreal experience.

Arriving in an almost empty car park, we thought the habit had not caught on in this part of France. In Britain, there would have been a healthy turnover of patrons enjoying a Double Bacon 'n' Egg McMuffin. Here the tables were barren and no sign of any staff. As we went to try the handle, my wife checked the opening time, then looked at her watch and saw it was five minutes short of mid-day.

Half an hour later and the car park and the place was full. Smartly dressed mothers were ushering their well-behaved children to tables and inspecting the menus as if they were in a three-star restaurant. There was a low hum of polite conversation, an absence of fat, tattooed people and not a single case of builder's bum. The decor, uniforms and familiar giant 'M' were all there, but it was different to any McDonald's we had visited anywhere else in the civilised world. To be fair, we have only ever been to three outlets, so perhaps we are not the best of judges.

Blaye

We have been caught almost unaware by what must be the end of our 400-mile journey.

Other travel writers have chosen different points at which to declare the death of the Dordogne, but we have chosen to go beyond their markers. This is not so much as wanting to be pioneers and establish new boundaries, but because we are loath to leave a friend who has given us such pleasure.

We have reached a point where all mention of the Dordogne has been dropped from our maps, and are now in the largest estuary in all France. It is coming up for fifty miles long and seven miles across its widest point. Short of taking to the waters and finding the spot where it starts to taste of brine, we have no way of knowing when the Dordogne gives up its individuality. But, by all accounts, Blaye seems as good a place as any to say goodbye.

For no good reason I can think of, the town reminds me of a small south coast resort like Worthing or Bognor. There is no pier at Blaye, nor any amusement arcades or fish and chip shops, but it has that same sort of air of a place providing a day out for those not looking for too much spectacle or excitement. There are some nice gardens along what could pass as a seafront, and some modest-looking hotels and bars and restaurants. Of most significance in the comparison with UK seaside daytrip favourites is the serried ranks of coaches filling the large car park. Next to the park is the impressive edifice which is clearly Blaye's major attraction.

The Verrou Vauban is an imposing and very substantial and imposing creation comprising two forts and an inner citadel. It is the result of a 17th-century demand by Louis XIV of his great naval architect to strengthen the existing fortifications on the estuary to protect Bordeaux from foreign incursions.

Sébastien Le Prestre Vauban was a Marshal of France

and the foremost military engineer of his age. His special talent was not only designing impregnable defences, but in machines for breaking through them. The Citadel was listed as a UNESCO World Heritage Site in 2008, and is nowadays assailed by many more visitors than ever tried to get through its giant gates in times of strife.

As it is the end of our journey we decide to splash out on accommodation, and set off in search of an English-speaking staff member at the tourist office.

*   *   *

As it happens, the staff at the Blaye Office de Tourisme all speak better English than me, and could not be more helpful. Unfortunately, they tell us, nearly every hotel, *chambres d'hotes* and other accommodation facility in the town is booked. There is a small hotel on the outskirts of town, but I can tell from the look on the nice young woman's face that it is not the sort of place she would like to send two wrinkly Brits.

*   *   *

My wife is insisting I check my flies and at least run my fingers through my hair, as we are about to spend our most expensive hotel night ever.

The last room at the cheap lodging place had been taken by the time we arrived. Back at the tourist office the nice lady had some good news. During our absence there was a last-minute cancellation at the hotel in the grand citadel. It has panoramic views across the estuary, his 'n' her toilets and wash basins, and the balcony overlooks the Olympic-sized swimming pool. Visitors would also find the finest quality complimentary chocolates on the designer pillow cases.

At this point and suspecting what was to come, I sat down and asked for the cost of a night in this temple of luxury accommodation. Tactfully, the young lady wrote the figure down and slipped it across the desk to me. I turned the piece of paper over, looked at it and then looked at it again as my eyes began to water. Then I gulped, nodded acceptance, shredded the piece of paper and prepared to lie to my wife. She would find out the cost in the morning when we used her card to pay, but by then it would be too late for her to veto spending more on a room for the night than an off-season package holiday in Greece.

*   *   *

It is nine pm and Blaye is officially shut for the night.

All along the strip overlooking the estuary, long-aproned waiters pile chairs on top of tables and glare menacingly at any passers-by who look as if they might want to come in. Last order time at all the restaurants has long gone, and we stand with our noses almost pressed to the glass looking at happy diners tucking in to seafood platters and assorted delights.

It is still possible to eat dinner at the hotel in which we are staying, but a quick look at the menu shows that the prices for eating are in line with the prices for sleeping there.

It is as we walk disconsolately down a side street that we become aware of a young man in a leather jacket, apparently guarding the entrance to an apartment block. It could be that he was standing outside to smoke a cigarette, but there is something shifty in the way he stands with collar turned up, looking each way along the street like a bookie's runner in the days before betting shops. He is not a big or intimidating person, and appears not so much a bouncer as a tout or even pimp.

As we draw level, he looks us up and down, takes a deep draw on his fag and beckons us over with a jerk of his head. Surely, I think, he is not going to invite a pair of aged Britons to join an illicit card game, or patronise an opium den or bordello?

It is with relief that I learn that he wants to know if we like Vietnamese food. We nod. He looks up and down the street again, and with another jerk of his head, beckons us follow him into the dimly-lit interior of the apartment block.

*   *   *

We have found ourselves in some unusual places during our years of wandering around France, but this is the first time I can remember sitting in a front room of someone's apartment while enjoying the best Vietnamese food I have ever tasted.

We are not the only diners, the set-up looks highly professional, so we wonder why the doorman acted as if he was offering forbidden delights. Perhaps the place is not fully licensed or should have ceased trading for the night, or perhaps it was just an unusual marketing ploy, but we are having a wonderful meal.

The owner is a small man of indeterminate age who walks with an increasingly pronounced limp as he continually returns to ply us with more food. After a few glasses of rice wine has loosened my tongue, I ask him how he came by the injury. He smacks his thigh resignedly and says it was during the fighting in Saigon in 1975. I do not like to ask which side he was on, but the way he fillets the fish he has brought to the table indicates he knows his way around an offensive weapon.

Two hours on and I have still not summoned up the nerve to ask our host about his time in Vietnam, but we have had a suitably magnificent meal to end our journey. We pay up and refuse yet another glass of rice wine (which I only recently noticed comes from a bottle in which sits a very large and hopefully dead scorpion) and stagger off back to our hotel.

Before turning in, we walk along the battlements of the citadel and look out across the estuary, trying to imagine what it would have been like to be on sentry go at the time in which it which it was built. A ferry sounds its mournful warning, and the lights on the far shore twinkle enticingly. We return to out balcony, I reach for the bottle of St

Émilion's finest and we think and talk about our journey.

It began where a trickle of water emerged from the side of an ancient volcano, working its sometimes tortuous way through so many different places and cultures before escaping into the sea.

By accompanying the Dordogne on its endless journey we have travelled not only through France, but also history. It has been a memorable and deeply rewarding trip, and a privilege to spend some time with one of the great rivers of Europe.

Recommended Reading

Constant and very welcome companions on our journey were three wayfarers who followed the course of the Dordogne more than a hundred years apart.

Three Rivers of France by Freda White (Faber and Faber) was first published in 1952, and covers the Lot and Tarn as well as the Dordogne. It has become a travel classic and as one critic said, wears its learning lightly.

Michael Brown published *Down the Dordogne* (Sinclair Stevenson) in 1991 after walking the four hundred miles from the river's source to Bordeaux. He writes in an amiable, non-fussy way and the book is packed with information about the history of the towns and villages occupying the banks of the Dordogne.

At the end of the 19th century Edward Harrison Barker went on the road to explore what was then known as Guyenne. He writes beautifully of the people and places encountered along the Dordogne as he effortlessly connects the distant past and present. We found his easy style, subtle humour and candid observations an absolute delight. The two books of his we took along the journey were *Two Summers in Guyenne* (*A chronicle of the Wayside and Waterside*) and *Wanderings by Southern Waters, Eastern Aquitaine*. Harrison is one of those rarest of travel writers - like Eric Newby - who actually make you feel you are at their side.

Finally, what we found particularly rewarding by reading these books was how much and yet how little the people and places along this great river have changed.

Other useful sources of written information were Val Gascoyne's *Dordogne/Lot*

(Lifeline) Jan Dodd's *Rough Guide to The Dordogne & the Lot*, and the *Michelin Dordogne Berry Limousin* guide. A good wheeze we employ when venturing into unknown territory is to throw ourselves on the mercy of the people living there. Useful websites with forums on which to ask for help include AngloINFO's Dordogne franchise (www.dordogne.angloinfo.com). Very helpful and detailed information about this part of France can be had from www.frenchentree.com

French Entree also offers some interesting regional recipes, particularly those from Amanda Lawrence. Amanda lives and works in the Quercy, surrounded by the vineyards of Cahors, and can be found on www.frenchvie.com

Some Fascinating Facts about the Author

Books written about France: 11

Magazine and newspaper articles about France: 827

Words written about France: 2,348,659 (approx)

Distance travelled in France: 678,962 miles (approx)

Regions visited: 22

Departments visited: 100

Fines for traffic/other offences: 9

Times eaten out in France: 2,456 (approx)

Bottles of wine drunk: 5,987 (very approx)

Times intoxicated by and in France: Innumerable

a taste of
French Impressions
Brittany

Did you know:

- *The crepe-throwing champion of all France is a Breton?*

- *The Klingon language is based on Breton...or the other way around?*

- *At midnight on Christmas Eve, all well water in Brittany turns to wine...but only for a few seconds?*

- *Breton authorities once blew up a seaside boulder because it looked like a penis?*

- *King Arthur and Merlin are said to be buried in seventeen different locations in the region, and The Holy Grail was first mentioned in a story set in Brittany?*

- *There is a Breton saint for every day of the year, which is why Bretons are such party animals?*

A bit like Wales. Not.

As we travel together through these pages, I shall try to get to grips with and pass on some aspects of the complex historical, cultural and geographical factors that have combined to make the region unique. In the meantime, here's a sort of Brittany Lite:

One of twenty-two *official regions of France, Brittany occupies the top left-hand corner of the country, and is often likened to Wales by British visitors and lazy travel writers like me. The comparisons are actually quite forgivable, as both are about the same size, and at four million-ish, have a similar population.

The landscape and weather are not dissimilar, with lots of hills, trees, water and rain. Although it might not appear so from a quick look at a map, the two places are not too far apart on length of coastline. Wales has 2120 kilometres of beaches, bays and cliffs, while at 2,730 km, Brittany claims a third of the total coastline of France. An additional factoid of interest to those who like to see the sea at regular intervals and without too much hassle is that nowhere in Brittany is further than fifty miles from the coast.

Like Wales, Brittany is very Celtic, though nobody seems quite sure why. In another parallel, the Breton language and separatist culture were discouraged and even suppressed by the French government until fairly recent times, though the former is making a comeback and the latter never went away.

Another echo is that a lot of foreigners have made their homes in Brittany. Unlike in some parts of Wales, the Anglo incomers have generally been made welcome, and especially if they can claim a smidgeon of Celtic genes. British incomers are popular as they bring much-needed money to the community pot, are generally fairly well-behaved, and often seen as less foreign than the French. Also and unlike in Wales, there has been no shortage of ruins for Brits to buy and do up. As most young Bretons would not dream of starting married life in a former cowshed with water running up as well as down the walls, there has been generally no more than a grade three shoulder shrug and a muted sigh of bemusement by the locals when confronted by what they see as a typically eccentric British penchant.

From a cultural perspective, Bretons appreciate greatly and like to practise art, particularly music. Two writers, three musicians, a sculptor and a bloke who makes life-sized blue plastic elephants just for fun live within a mile of where we were based in the mountains of Finistère. And that's with a population density not much above the most unfashionable areas of the Gobi Desert.

As further evidence of loving art for no more than its own sake, where else in France (or the rest of Europe) would hard-nosed farmers spend the time and trouble to make artistic *tableaux* from hay bales in their roadside fields just so that passers-by can enjoy them?

A final and, I think, significant statistic about Brittany is that the region boasts more independent (i.e. small and privately-owned) breweries than the rest of France put together. This is just one more reason we found ourselves so much at home here.

* The exact boundaries, number and even names of the regions of France are often contested, and mostly by those who live in them.

Home cooking

As every non-biased observer knows, the French are-or like to appear-very fussy about their food. Unlike their liberal attitudes towards all matters sexual and things like farting and peeing in public, they are narrow-minded and even prudish about what may or may not be put in one's mouth in the food line. Some would say they are obsessed with being accepted as the arbiter, authority and even originator of all dishes worth eating. Who else but the French would name the humble cottage pie after the man they say invented it?

I find attitudes refreshingly different in this region; Bretons seem much more down to earth and modest about their cuisine. I am sure lots of people from other regions would say they have much to be modest about.

While the coastal areas are known for dishing up anything that comes from the sea and moves (and quite a lot of things which do not), inland Breton cuisine seems based mainly on bread and butter and salt. Or rather flour and butter and salt. The wallpaper paste Madame gave me for helping with her horses was in fact a standard *crêpe* mixture. The brown brick was *bouille d'avoine*, a regional delicacy used to make what we would call gruel.

In the old days, Breton peasants would gather round a cauldron bubbling with *yod kerc'h*, or oats and water. When it was judged ready, the head of the household would make a hole in the sludge and add a lump of butter. There would then be a free-for-all to see who could get a spoonful from the buttery bit. This slap-up treat would be washed down with *lez ribot*, a Breton variety of buttermilk, and on holy and high days a glass of cider might be added to the pot.

Nowadays, *bouille d'avoine* is sold as a luxury item in supermarkets with specially reinforced shelves. I am told Breton gourmets (which seems a bit of an oxymoron) fry it with sesame seeds, but I reckon it would be more suitable for repairing the soles of clogs.

Unlike the residents of most other regions, Bretons like their butter salted, and a number of traditional recipes recommend eye-wateringly and artery-clogging amounts. For some reason Brittany was exempted from a tax on salt right up till the Revolution, which is perhaps why Bretons have always been so liberal in its usage. Predictably, there was also a healthy trade in salt smuggling across the border.

The basic Breton *crêpe* is, for all the fuss some people make about it, no more than a thin pancake of buckwheat flour. These were made by literally whipping the batter by hand, then cooking both sides on a flat stone or a rimless cast-iron pan called a *bilig*.

Although crêpe is the familiar generic name, in Brittany it is generally limited to pancakes with sweet fillings, while the savoury versions are called *galettes*. Arguments rage about the exact type of flour mix or type to use for either variety, but I do not want to get into that angels-on-a-pinhead type of debate as life is far too short. Galette is also a term used for flat cakes or other confections, but that is another place I do not wish us to go. Suffice it to say that Bretons will put almost anything savoury in a galette, and the Breton version of a bacon and egg sarnie can be bought at most markets; the knack of eating one without decorating your shirt front is a skill which marks out locals from visitors.

The knack of making such an apparently simple thing as a crêpe/galette also takes a bit of acquiring. If the mixure is too thinly spread in the pan it will break up when you try to turn your nascent crêpe over or remove it from the pan; if you have put too much batter in the pan, it will be rubbery when it comes out. Do not depair if your early attempts do not work out well, as we have found that practice does make perfect; If I can make a proper-tasting and looking crêpe, anyone with two hands can.

Should you fancy trying your hand at knocking up a bunch of basic galettes/crêpes, here's a typical recipe. In Brittany it is usual to make a big batch of around 30 pancakes, so be sure to invite some friends along to try them (or adjust the measures accordingly):

Ingredients:

6 ounces of wheat flour

1lb of buckwheat flour

3 eggs

5 oz salted, melted butter

Half a bottle of dry cider (approximately a pint)

2 litres of milk (go on, use full-fat just this once)

Some cold water and fresh or packet yeast.

A teaspoonful of salt

Method

Put the flour into a mixing bowl and break the eggs into a well in the centre. Start mixing the batter with a wooden spoon (or your fist if you want to be faithful to the original recipe) and gradually add the milk and cider. Finish off by adding some water (if necessary) and the yeast, but beware of making the batter too runny. Melt half the butter and add to the mixture. Find a suitable flat stone, or failing that, gently heat a small frying pan which has been greased with some cooking oil. When the pan is really hot, ladle enough batter in to cover the surface of the pan. Leave for a couple of minutes or until the surface starts to bubble, then turn over and lavish some more butter on it.

N.B. keep the mixture beaten between the making of each crêpe. You are now ready to experiment with fillings, which should be enclosed in the galette so that the finished article resembles a deflated Cornish pasty.

Sporting note

Thankfully for the maintenance of world peace, the record for galette throwing is held by a Breton. Along with apricot stone spitting and beret tossing, new attempts on the crêpe-chucking record take place at the small town of Mahalon each July, but so far no-one has come near to equalling the tally of 7.45 metres established in 2000 by local hero Fabien Le Coz.

Dietary concerns

A common Breton recipe for long life and good health comes out as *debri mad*, *kousel mad*, *kaohad mad*. In keeping with their view of the important things in life (after art and drinking), the maxim translates as 'eating well, sleeping well, shitting well...'

MAY

Huelgoat, Le Cloître St-Thégonnec,
the lake at Brennilis,
the chapel of St Michel at Brasparts,
St-Jean-Trolimon , Lake Guerlédan, Bon Repos,
Les Forges des Salles, Mur-de-Bretagne,
Pontivy, Loudéac

All the auguries promise a fruitful summer. Nature has obviously followed to the letter her own recipe for the mix of rain and sun at just the right times, and the verges and hedgerows are aglow with verdant colour. There are swelling seas of dandelions and oceans of buttercups yellowly lining the lanes around our new home, and the pinewood copse is carpeted with harebells mingling with the modest beauty of Solomon's-seal. Taken together with other indicators like the stiffness of our nearest neighbour's left elbow, these colourful displays are flagging up the promise of good times to come.

In the meantime, we have been taking up our indulgent landlady's invitation to make ourselves at home on her land. The deal is that we will keep an eye on the grounds, plants, streams, mini-lake and woodland and in return may make reasonable use of the terrain for our crops and animals. The distant owner of these premises is a keen gardener and animal lover, and obviously likes the idea that her land will be put to fitting purpose. A good deal is when both sides are content, so I think we have struck a very good deal indeed by choosing to rent Paradise for a year.

A vegetable garden has been dug and fenced off, and a contented quartet of chickens are sizing up their new surroundings and each other to see who is going to be at the top of the pecking order. So far my money is on the little Sussex Red. As in human societies, it is often the smallest and noisiest who emerge as leaders and sometimes dictators.

We have never lived in the countryside without keeping chickens, and do not see how we could be without their company. I once worked out that each egg from our hens costs more than a dozen from most supermarkets, but this way we know not only when they arrived, but how. And illusory as it probably is, they taste so much better straight from the hen.

We picked the four birds up at a local market yesterday after I had made them a luxurious home in the old stables alongside the barn. Donella is fussing around the new arrivals like, well, a mother hen, and has already given them suitable names. The warlike Sussex Red is now to be known as Brunhilde, the large and placid speckled grey is Griselda, the huge white and obviously soppy bird will be known as Blanche, while we have called the black one Whitney. This is not only because of her colour, but because she is already showing signs of divadom and likes to make peculiar movements with her beak whilst squawking.

*   *   *

Night comes slowly in this elevated area, and there is a luminous quality to the light as I sit beneath the ancient *calvaire* which marks the boundaries of the hamlet and the beginning of the track up to the moors and mountains.

It is unlikely there is a settlement in Brittany which did not have one of these sombre stone creations, clearly erected to remind the inhabitants that they and their behaviour were being watched. This one may have a particular significance, as a great battle between the forces of good and evil is said to have been fought on this spot a thousand years and more ago. The remaining bits of the slain good guys were taken to a holy place nearby, which is where the abbey of Le Relec got its name. Or, of course, the story might be a lot of codswallop, dreamed up by our neighbour or the Finistère Tourist Board of 1347.

Curiously, though they are decidedly Christian in intent, some of the most unfussy and even primitive-looking calvaires have a pagan, polytheistic feel. If not topped with minimalistic crosses, they may display complex Celtic-style stone knots or gargoyle-like faces, and I have seen one with what looks like a pair of spread buttocks mooning at passers-by. Brittany has more calvary crosses than anywhere else in France, and the oldest is in the south Finistère town of St-Jean-Trolimon. The level of intricacy and stone filigree work on a calvaire normally denotes the alleged piety level of the inhabitants, and it is interesting that the one we sit beneath is almost totally devoid of frills and curlicues. The base is made of large, roughly-dressed blocks, from which rises a central column. There is some small detail at the top, but centuries of moorland weather have made it unrecognisable. The base is a good place to rest after a walk across the moors, and the blocks are comfortably indented from the wear and tear of ten thousand bottoms.

My reverie is interrupted by the pained roar of a mistreated engine, and a battered Range Rover lurches around the bend of the track leading to the neighbouring hamlet of Kernelec. It is strange how intrusive is the noise of a car in this pastoral setting, while a tractor roaring by is just an agreeable part of the rural scene.

I am particularly irked by the intrusion as the passer-by is Lady Muck. She is the daughter of the elderly couple who presented me with the brown brick on our first night here, but appears not to approve of the presence of outsiders on her territory. It says much about her view of her status that she drives a vehicle more associated with haughty county and country ladies in Britain than French hill farmers.

Lady Muck and her husband farm most of the surrounding fields, and because generations of her family have lived on and off the land here, she seems to regard the two hamlets and network of lanes and tracks as part of her private estate. This is not an uncommon attitude, and also why it is rarely a good idea to buy a spare house or barn from a farmer who is going to continue working and living nearby. Many forget about the money they got for their former property, and thus view the new owners as squatters.

Wanting us to be seen as friendly and unthreatening incomers, I tried waving and smiling when the lady of this manor first bucketed by, but that seemed to make her even more unhappy. Then my friendly wave changed to a two fingered version when she refused to acknowledge us beyond a curt nod. Now, when she passes I sweep off my hat, tug my forelock and make an exaggerated bow, but I think the irony is lost on her. Once I contrived to be peeing into a hedge as she approached, and turned as if by accident as she passed. There was no more than a flicker of acknowledgement, and I thought I detected a look of condescending pity before remembering she owns a prize bull and keeps an awesomely-equipped Breton shire horse in her top field.

Now the coast is clear, I walk along the lane and over the hump-back bridge to leave a handful of dried dog food under a hazel bush. Since we got the chickens, I have been trying to establish a telepathic rapport with the local fox so we can come to an agreement. The basic conditions of the compact are that I will provide breakfast and dinner each day, and he or she or members of the immediate family will not eat our hens.

I know the locals would think me deranged, which is why I leave the food when there is nobody about. But I believe I can establish sympathetic contact, and so far our contract has been upheld. The fox will certainly know there are chickens in the area, as someone at Kernelec keeps a cockerel and this is the best advertisement for the presence of hens. We have not met yet, but I and my dog have felt his presence at dusk. Last week I saw a flash of grey in the woods above the lane, and have never seen Milly react so dramatically to a fox. Although the locals would consider me mad for even thinking it, it is just possible that there is a wolf living in the pine forest at the foot of the moors. Books were written as recently as 1875 about the pleasures of wolf-hunting in the Black Mountains*, and that massive ridge of slate lies directly to the south. On the other side of the moorlands and at the gateway of the Monts d'Arrée, Le Cloitre St-Thégonnec has cornered the wolf fascination market. An impressive stone carving of a family of wolves sits at the heart of the village, and there is a museum devoted to the history, biology and legends surrounding the species' activity in Brittany. The reason Le Cloitre feels entitled to be the authority on all things wolf-like is that the last recorded killing of one in the Arrée mountains was by villager Pierre Berrehar on the 6th of October 1884.

Whether because of its location or the nature of its localised claim to historical fame, the village certainly has a timeless feel about it. There is a very good bakery and grocery shop, and a classic rural bar tabac and eating place run by a young, single and attractive woman. This may account for its popularity as a gathering place for men of all ages. A more debatable issue why Le Cloitre has one of the best-maintained and preserved churches in the area, yet like all other smaller places of worship hereabouts, it will be closed on Sunday. In a very Roman Catholic region of France, this is a puzzle, especially when one sees the church brooding sulkily and the bar across the square packed to the doors.

* *Wolf-Hunting and Wild Sport in Lower Brittany by EWL Davies is a rollicking read and a freely available digital copy is to be found at:*
www.archive.org/details/wolfhuntingwilds00davirich

Thursday 1st

Today is a public holiday, or rather *the* public holiday. Curiously, only May 1st (Labour Day) is on the statute books as an official day off for all French workers. The rest are granted by what is called a collective convention, and the convention often seems to be that there are more days off than on. Few saints are forgotten when it comes to looking for an excuse to take a break from work, and a popular device is 'the bridge'. This comes into play when there is a public holiday anywhere near a weekend and it is not deemed worth going back to work for the day or two in between the official day off and the nearest Saturday or Sunday.

The total for time away from work for most French people over the course of a year takes no account of sickness (the French are demonstrably the most enthusiastic hypochondriacs in Europe) and the standard five weeks holiday in the summer. Nor do the statistics take into account all the strikes and unofficial stoppages.

Because it is not only public servants and people working for big companies who enjoy public holidays, nearly all shops and many bars and restaurants and other places of entertainment will be closed, leaving those on a day off with nothing to do away from home. This is perhaps why there is a law banning the use of mowers on public holidays, and why everyone with a garden ignores it.

Saturday 3rd

Elsewhere in France, the Monts d'Arrée would be seen as little more than hilly ground, but Bretons like to make the most of their natural assets. Anyway, the moors and craggy tors surrounding our new home have more to offer than mere height above sea level.

In keeping with the Breton love of myth, mystery and supernaturality, this is the kingdom of Ankou (literally 'Mister Death') the aforementioned reaper of souls. Here also be any number of mischievous sprites and will o' the wisps, including whole tribes of vengeful trouble-making hobgoblins called Korrigans.

Running in a north-easterly slant and punctuated by giant granite outcrops, this rugged part of the Breton landscape forms the border between the ancient areas of Léon and Cornouaille. From the top of the highest crag above Lesmenez, one can see toy-like ferry boats steaming in and out of harbour at Roscoff, and, on an especially clear day, waves crashing against the cliffs of the Pink Granite coast. From this vantage point, there is also much evidence of the diversity and sometimes breathtakingly monumental style of the Breton landscape. A couple of miles to the south is the great lake at Brennilis, surrounded by some of the oldest and biggest peat bogs in Europe. At a mile across and more than a thousand acres in surface area, Brennilis matches a fair-size Scottish loch or Cumbrian mere. The lake was once claimed (probably by a rival commune) to be the watery path to the gates to Hell. This may also be why they built the now redundant nuclear reactor on its shores.

Further afield towards the town of Brasparts is the tiny chapel of St Michel, sitting atop what is thought to be a giant Celtic tumulus and approached from one side with a step for nearly every day of the year.

They farm high in this part of Brittany, and patchwork fields of rape and cereal share the rugged terrain with peat bogs, scrubby gorse and pastureland. The county of Finistère is big on beef and dairy cattle, but there is a curious absence of sheep. According to our nearest neighbour, this is because they cannot survive wet and cold winter conditions.

Alain LeGoff has obviously never visited Wales, and we are told that the real reason sheep are not kept here is because there is little money in raising them. Not that I would suggest this to our neighbour, as after twenty years of close encounters I think I know how to best handle aged French countrymen, especially the unmarried variety.

Growing up in an isolated community free of television and cars and most other outside influences must obviously have an effect on the individual's character and philosophy. Certainly, it seems to me that all the older French countrymen I have met share some commonalities. While apparently innocent or at least unknowing of the ways of the modern world, they seem to compensate by developing a level of cunning which would make a particularly crafty fox jealous. Bachelors are the most extreme of the genre, and invariably rigidly fixed in their ways and views. Even when they don't, they have an unshakeable belief that they know all there is to know about the countryside, and that your originating from any town or part of Britain will guarantee you to be completely clueless about all rural matters.

Our nearest neighbour is a little over eighty, and is thus the youngest permanent resident of the hamlet. He was born in Lesmenez and lives alone in a small house behind his impressively distressed ancestral farmhouse, which has been uninhabited and uninhabitable for the best part of a century. Alain helped his father build the new house when he was ten, and the granite blocks were brought by wagon the twelve rocky miles across the mountains from the quarry at Huelgoat.

We met the day after our arrival, when I thought I had surprised an off-piste Korrigan in the copse by the pond. Then the figure emerged from the undergrowth and I saw that, except for the footwear, he was wearing standard French aged countryman's outfit. Topping off a face with the texture of a well-weathered Cox's pippin was the inevitable time-shiny cloth cap which would probably take a surgical operation to remove, and below the neckline was the usual ensemble of tightly-buttoned suit jacket over collarless shirt and extremely lived-in trousers. This being Brittany, the footwear was specific to the region, with carpet slippers sheathed in traditional wooden clogs. The only thing missing was the roll-up cigarette welded to the lower lip.

As we should have expected, our nearest neighbour seems unaware of any boundaries or town-grown taboos on dropping in unannounced and is apt to appear like a pantomime genie at any time and anywhere. So far he has not materialised in the bed or bathroom or toilet while we have been using them, but it can only be a matter of time. Though the sudden manifestations can be a little unnerving and even dangerous when I am using a chain saw or halfway up a ladder or both, we like the informality, and the open-door policy also applies to his domain.

Yesterday, Alain materialised in our kitchen as we were trying to relieve the suffering of an ailing hen. Griselda went off lay last week, and it is pitiful to hear her keening cry as she lies forlornly and eggless in the nesting box. As she grew more and more moribund and miserable, a visit to the vet confirmed she was egg-bound and we were offered three solutions. The first, said the affably honest Mr Tanguy, was to buy from him an exceptionally expensive ointment to ease the passage for the egg from inside to outside Griselda. The second would be to try the undignified but sometimes more effective ruse of holding her over a pan of boiling water so that the steam would act as a lubricant. The third and most obvious solution would be to cut our losses and eat her.

It was while I held poor Griselda above the steaming pot and Donella pulled on her rubber gloves that Alain made his entry. For a moment, we held the silent tableau, then before leaving to report the weird goings-on to the rest of the village, he cleared his throat, gave a mini-shrug and observed dryly that, in France, though people like their food as fresh as possible, it is considered normal to kill and pluck a chicken before cooking it.

Huelgoat

From his bar stool, Clint Eastwood surveys his surroundings with that trademark part-puzzled, fully angry squint. At his shoulder, a man with a purple head is arguing with himself about whose turn it is to buy the next round. From a nearby table the mad monk Rasputin is giving us the evil eye.

On the terrace, a coach-load of tourists is pretending to be entertained by a man wearing a monogrammed dressing-gown and an oversized pair of boxing gloves. He ducks and feints and shuffles adroitly as they smile weakly in a very English way. What they do not know is that the man is reprising the action on the night he claims he nearly won the area finals in the Breton boxing championships of 1976. The locals know he is a former Latin teacher, and some say he lost his reason trying to conjugate a particularly ticklish irregular verb for his bored pupils. The more cynical say he is merely a compulsive attention seeker and very mean, and that he wears the boxing gloves so as to be unable to get his hands in his pocket when it is his turn to buy a round.

From what we have learned, this is just another average night in Huelgoat. It is our first official run ashore, and we have obviously come to the right place for local colour and interesting characters. Armed with some stunning natural attributes, a few made-up legends and lots of places to take drink, Huelgoat is a very popular tourist attraction. Huelgoatians also clearly like a drink, as for a static population of only a thousand there are seventeen licensed premises which remain open all year round. As well as the facilities in the betting shop and camping gaz outlet, there are even well-appointed bars in the two bakeries in case customers become faint with thirst while waiting for their daily baguette.

Claims to fame for Huelgoat ('High woods' in Breton) include a large lake, hundreds of acres of forests ringing the town, a world-renowned arboretum and a fascinating valley trail called The Chaos. This forest and riverside walk is littered with giant rocks said to be thrown around when the giant Pantagruel stubbed his toe and lost his cool while passing through. I reckon it more likely he was staggering home after a night on the batter in Huelgoat and felt like a bit of full-on giant-sized vandalism.

Like a hundred others around Europe and even further afield, the town also claims to be a favourite stopping-off place for King Arthur, with the alleged remains of his camp to be found high in the forest. Later and more verifiable residents of note include the ancestors of American Beat Generation poet, novelist and artist Jack Kerouac. Impressionist painter Paul Gauguin is said to have painted the lake from the attic studio above a shop just off the square, but as the premises sells painting and art materials that could be a marketing ploy. TV archeologist Sir Mortimer Wheeler often dug here, and it is a much-told story that actress Jane Fonda once cooked a crêpe for her then boyfriend Roger Vadim in the kitchen of a hotel in the square.

Pagan groups are said to prance regularly around in the forest, and it is claimed by those who also claim to know about these things that Huelgoat sits on a confluence of ley lines, giving it a mystical significance and special appeal to people of a spiritual nature. This may actually be true, and I do believe there is something special about the town. It might be the force of nature, or it could just be the number and variety of bars on tap which attracts so many unusual people. Huelgoat certainly seems to have its fair share of weirdos, which is why my wife says I feel so instantly at home here.

Our guide and future gossip correspondent for this part of the region is Allan Bevan, a former naval master-at-arms in the Royal Navy who now runs a bed and breakfast establishment near the square. Or rather, his wife Ann runs the B&B, while Allan absorbs the ambience and red wine and researches the book he will one day write about his life and times in Huelgoat. As he says, if and when it is done it will have to go in the fiction department, as nobody would believe it to be about real people and circumstances.

As the evening revs up, we learn that, as usual in situations like these in rural France, all is not as it seems at first sight. Clint Eastwood is actually a local plumber who has long tried and failed to make a living as a lookalike of the rangy Hollywood star. I am puzzled by his lack of success as, unlike nearly all lookalikes I have seen, he really is the spitting image of Eastwood during his *Dirty Harry* years. Then Claude/Clint climbs down from his stool, disappears from sight behind it, and his severe lack of inches explains the reason for his lack of bookings.

As Allan explains, the man with the purple head is a local artist who enjoys the company of an imaginary friend, while the mad monk is a former car sprayer and now part-time Druid who lives in a caravan in the forest with-he claims-a tribe of Breton wood elves. The reason for the baleful stare is apparently that we have not taken out the insurance cover offered to British visitors which involves buying him a drink to avoid their holiday being cursed.

As to the size of the crowd, the reason the bar is so busy is that the premises are under new management.

The locals have turned out in force to check out such important issues as the ease and level of credit rating and what the new patrons are made of, and Madame is doing her best to show them. She would be tall even without her towering stiletto heels, and is wearing a very unpractical and flimsy dress which clearly leaves very little room for underwear. What looks like Christmas tree baubles hang from her ears, but all male attention is focused on the spheres struggling to escape from the plunging neckline of her blouse. Each time she leans forward to attend to a customer, there is an appreciable stiffening in the bar and a sudden falling off of conversation. Allan says a sweepstake has already been set up to estimate the exact date and time her breasts will escape from their billet, and other side wagers include estimating their individual and combined dimensions and weight. To get some inside information, one of the local sculptors has offered to create a life-size statue of her to go in the bar window, but her husband has said he would prefer it to be a bust. Allan points to where a middle-aged man is leaning on the bar, obviously studying form. He must be favourite for winning one of the side bets, says our host, as he is the owner of the town grocery store and renowned for his ability to gauge weight without the aid of a pair of scales.

*   *   *

We have been enjoying a very Breton rite of spring at the hamlet which looks down on the rooftops of Lesmenez. Kernelec is a bigger and racier dwelling place than ours as there are more than a dozen residents and some are below retirement age. Lady Muck lives here, as does the sculptor whose life-sized plastic elephant guards the border between us and them.

We are venturing into rival territory because we have befriended an English couple who have a holiday home in Kernelec. Their little stone cottage is everything one would hope for in its eye-pleasingness, and made more attractive by the sorely distressed property across the lane. The man who lives in it is clearly someone who likes to start projects and not finish them. Since we arrived, his cottage seems to become ever more distressed as bits are knocked down and not replaced. Even he has realised the threat of an imminent collapse, and the plastic elephant has recently been shifted to help support the sagging gable. This rearrangement has started a promising village feud, as the lady of the cottage opposite says she resents waking each morning to look out of her window and up an elephant's arse. Tonight she will be happy, as the blue elephant has been moved to provide a static ride for local children. Our dusk piper has been performing, and still cannot get the tune of the regional anthem right. The elephant man is putting on a marionette show, and guest of honour will be an exhibition of impromptu Morris dancing, put on by the holiday home-owning Brits. They are an unusual couple, even for these parts. With a suitably Dickensian name, Morley Friend is a man of huge size and heart, and with his rumpled, baggy clothing and giant, slow moving amiable bulk, he brings to mind the elephant across the road. He is clearly a man whose depth, sensitivity and understanding of the world match his size, though he likes to pretend otherwise. His sensitivity is probably why he so often hangs his head and sighs at the ironies and perversities of life and follies of Man and the former Milk Marketing Board.

Sue Friend could come from Central Casting as an apple-cheeked farmer's wife, and is as small and straightforward as her husband is vast and complex. The couple are dairy farmers who live in a remote part of Devon, and are in the painful process of handing the running of the farm over to their son. Upcott Farm has been in Friend hands for five generations and as retirement age approaches, it is time for Morley to step back. His health is not good, and like many vigorous and powerful men, he resents bitterly the depredations of age. Last week he let out a gale of a sigh, shook his great shaggy head and told me that if he were one of his own animals he would shoot himself.

Sunday 11th

I have misjudged Lady Muck. Far from being stuck up and xenophobic, she is just shy. She also does not like the job which occupies almost all her waking hours, which explains her preoccupied and distant air when she races by. Mary-Jo arrived at the kitchen door yesterday to see if we would like to buy a stake in one of her soon-to-be slaughtered steers. She was taking orders in advance, and would put our name on any parts not already spoken for. When I persuaded her to come in and risk an English coffee, she became quite talkative. After I had remarked how many people would envy her life, she said they might find it not as bucolically attractive as in slushy films and novels. Mary-Jo is the only child of Mr and Mrs Goarnisson, and felt she had no choice but take over the farm when her parents reached official retirement age. Contrary to what a lot of civilians think, she said, spending one's life up to the ankles in cow shit is not all it is cracked up to be. Waving as she drove off and back to a life she resents, I thought how easily we make assumptions based on our own beliefs or prejudices. When you are also communicating in a language which is foreign to one of you, it is even easier to jump to the wrong conclusions.

Monday 12th

We have been visiting the next-door department of Côtes d'Armor to view an isolated farmhouse and its almost inevitable gite 'complex' (usually code for one other building apart from the owners' accommodation). The premises are up for sale, and the indulgence of a spare designer home which nobody lives in may well be the reason.

A major challenge for many Britons buying a wreck in France is to discover how expensively they can turn the former pig sty, cattle byre or other unsuitable ruin into a guest house which will cost more to do up than it could earn from visitors in two lifetimes. I believe the real reason most Britons spend so much on gites is not because they believe them to be a commercial proposition, but so the women can have even more bathrooms and toilets to not use. I have noticed how the number of bathrooms in their new homes seems to be of increasingly crucial importance to British owners, and it is not uncommon for them to total more than the bedroom count. The property we are looking at has four bedrooms, five bathrooms, a shower room and three separate toilets. Apart from having become a place of thanksgiving to the local plumber, the property is said to be a real bargain; this usually means it will not be for some undisclosed reason, but for us the journey is a good excuse to take the measure of the surrounding countryside.

Finistère is often likened to Cornwall, while Côtes

d'Armor's undulating hills, vales and less dramatically craggy coastline calls Devon or Dorset to mind. It is a place of rolling green sward, fenceless fields and ancient deciduous woods and forests. This glorious setting naturally makes it a favourite buying place for Brits who think they would like to live in a place which reminds them of how they think England used to look. Côtes d'Armor also has the appeal of being the cheapest department for property, for which I have been unable to discover any other reason than common-or-garden snobbery.

From what we have seen, the views and coastline and weather and other pro and con factors in this department equal if not surpass those in the other three, but just as in Britain, unfathomable fashion sets the agenda and the house prices. It is interesting how Britons take their tribal prejudices and preferences with them, even or especially when buying or moving abroad. On the boat from Portsmouth, a slightly drunk property agent told me he could always tell in which part of Brittany his British customers would buy just by looking at the make and vintage of their cars. Those pulling up in a convertible BMW or similarly flash car would most likely choose the coastal area of Morbihan, or swisher parts of Ille-et-Vilaine. Couples from the north of Britain who arrived in battered vans would like the look of property prices in Côtes d'Armor, while those crusty Brits favouring beards, lived-in clothing and even more lived-in Volvo estates would always be taken with Finistère. When I asked him where he thought we were bound for, he said my beard and decaying body-warmer were a dead giveaway, and he bet we had a Volvo on the car deck and were heading for the furthest reaches of the end of the earth. He was spot-on, but we also like the look of Côtes d'Armor, and especially the property prices.

Whatever we think of the farmhouse which is up for sale, it seems we will be spoiled for choice across the whole region. Thousands of very expensively restored and improved properties have recently been put up for sale by Britons who have realised that living in a foreign country is not for them. Sadly it is a common and usually very costly mistake to think it would be even better to live full time in a place that you love visiting for a couple of weeks a year.

There are a number of factors causing the current Dunkirk-like retreat of so many expatriate or second home-owning Britons. Some Brits are going home for purely financial reasons, which can be fairly blamed on the current recession. Others would have committed fiscal hara-kiri at any time by coming over to buy a modest holiday home then borrowing shedloads of foreign money for a much bigger and more expensive place.

Then there are those who fled to France to escape the bad bits about life in Britain only to discover how much they miss the good bits. There is no shame in finding that you do not like living in a foreign land, but it has become taboo for expatriates to admit it to other people - or even themselves. Health reasons or missing friends and family are the most common excuses for retreating Brits, and I know of those who have claimed marital breakdown rather than admit they just don't like living in France or with the French.

The couples who seem most successful in adapting to and even relishing living with the old enemy are those with strong relationships, enquiring minds and a generally philosophical outlook. Most valuable of all is a sense of humour and proportion, especially when accepting how differently and sometimes even badly things are done in your host country.

*   *   *

We will not be putting in an offer for the farmhouse. If the place was restored by British craftsmen, I think they must have been graduates of the Channel Crossing University of Construction. It is a standing joke that there is an office on board all ferry boats to Brittany and other French ports which offers instant certification in all building trades. Whether or not this is true, many Britons who wish to start a new working life in France board the ferry as graphic designers, car dealers, lorry drivers or aromatherapists, then disembark as allegedly expert plumbers, carpenters and general builders. I have seen some extreme examples of their work, and still have bad dreams.

Strangely, I have also seen even grosser acts of vandalism practiced by the people who own the properties than the dodgy Brit builders they might have employed. For while the instant converts to builderdom learn the ropes on other people's properties, some British home owners are happy to practice on their own. It can be traumatic for the visitor to see what horrors can be wrought by an enthusiastic amateur whose previous experience in DIY has been limited to screwing a shelf to a wall. Curiously, most of those afflicted by the compulsion to Do It Themselves Very Badly are, like the parents of ugly children, unable to see their handiwork as others do.

Apart from the appalling and often lethal standard of the work, the property we visited was not ideally located. Instantly identifiable as British-owned by its silly name, *Les Deux Tournesols* stands just up the road from a busy pig-rearing and slaughtering facility, though the owner assured us it is only noticeable when the wind comes from the east or the carcass lorry goes by every Thursday. Also, he felt obliged to point out that the garden behind the property belonged to someone in the next village who had gone on record as saying he would never sell it. What the owner's wife thought of their new home and life in rural France we could not tell, as the man looked wistfully out of the window for a while before saying she was in England visiting family and friends.

Sadly, this, as we have already learned, is often expat code for 'She's left me...'

*   *   *

Driving through a small town this morning I had to take to the pavement to avoid a vehicle charging out from a minor side road. It was coming from the right, so I was in the wrong. Had there been a stop sign, the driver would have been required to heave to and wait till the main road was clear before entering it. As the minor road was little more than an alleyway, had no cautionary markings and was virtually concealed by the communal Christmas tree which had been obviously kept and put there for camouflage purposes, the driver was entirely in his rights to charge out and dare me to collide with him.

This is because, in the land of Descartes, Simone de Beauvoir and a host of other big-hitting philosophers and allegedly logical thinkers, there exists an ancient yet unrepealed driving law so bizarre that even French drivers generally ignore it unless they are in a really bloody mood.

In essence, the law requires any 40 tonne Euro-lorry barrelling down a main road to give way to any vehicle emerging from any minor passageway to the right. As if the old *Priorité à Droite* code was not crazy enough, it also applies to some roundabouts. Not all, but some. In effect, that means that you have to give way to traffic *joining* one of these roundabouts rather than vehicles already on it. The situation is further complicated by most French drivers ignoring or not knowing the law, but others calling it into play depending on the situation, local custom and the driver's mood at that moment.

Officially, any communes exercising their right to employ the old priority-to-the-right ruling must say so in the form of a prominently displayed notice. In fact, most are carefully hidden or placed in the most obscure positions, to be seen only after the visitor has passed through the danger zone. The advice given to foreign drivers is to be prepared to respect the current priority usage when on a main road, but not to expect others to respect it when they are coming out of a side road. In the case of this morning's incident, the attacking vehicle was an ambulance. It could be that the driver was a stickler for tradition, that the mayor of this town has decided to observe the old law on alternate weekdays, or that the ambulance was merely touting for trade.

Lake Guerlédan

The jewel in the tourist crown of Côtes d'Armor, Lake Guerlédan is the largest stretch of inland water in Brittany, and looks it. Its electricity-generating powers were created in the 1930s by flooding the valley where the Nantes to Brest canal meets the Blavet river. Together with four hundred hectares of woodland, a number of houses and lock-keeper's cottages were swallowed up in the process, providing an ideal opportunity for local tourist officials and other interested parties to hint at ghostly sights and sounds emanating from beneath the waters. More credible stories surround the founding of the Cistercian abbey of Bon Repos, which sits alongside the canal at the western end of Lake Guerlédan. Here are staged regular regional events and sometimes really spectacular *son et lumière* spectacles. Close by, Les Forges des Salles is in a much better state of preservation, and was an entire village devoted to the art and practice of blacksmithery. Surrounding the lake and its miles of walks and cycle tracks is one of the biggest private forests in Brittany.

Facing the ruined abbey on the other side of the canal is what comes close in my book to being the perfect bar. Until last year it was owned by an eccentric (even for Brittany) Breton who made a unilateral declaration of independence and claimed his bar to be the official hostelry of the principality of Bon Repos. I do not think there were any tax, duty free or other advantages to the scheme, as he opened and shut exactly when he liked and seemed completely immune to infection by modern customer service principles.

We thought he would be a very hard act to follow, but the new owners are equally as eccentric in a different way. Madame restricts her self-expression mainly to purple hair and some beguiling combinations of short skirts and heavy boots, but the patron is particularly interesting. Working from a kitchen alongside and no bigger than the unisex toilet, he offers hundreds of dishes and daily specials, each with his own signature styling. He also demonstrates his artistic sensibilities by a penchant for white see-through tops and trousers, and, set free, his hair would reach his waist. He also smokes a cigarette more creatively than any Frenchman I have seen, and that is saying something. Unusually for a rural French bar, he also serves snacks. On our last visit, my wife's slice of *gâteau de fromage blanc* was garnished with a segment of tangerine, three sculpted grapes, two currants and a drizzle of raspberry sauce. Sticking in the top as the *pièce de résistance* was something like a miniature cheerleader's razzle-stick.

Although a pale imitation of British-bred cheesecake in taste, it was a rare treat, as the serving of snacks in many rural French bars is regarded by their owners as akin to dealing in class 'A' drugs. It is my wife's theory that the disinterest in coffee and cake breaks is what keeps older French women so noticeably slim, and examples of their abstinence are everywhere. There is a very traditional Breton bar and restaurant in the grounds of Le Relec, and each day of the summer dozens of coaches laden with mostly middle-aged or older ladies arrive in the car park. After walking around the abbey and grounds, the ladies push their way past the seating outside the bar and climb on board the coach. In England, there would be quite intense hand-to-hand fighting to win a place at table for the holy rite and right of huge slices of carrot and cheesecake with a cup of tea or coffee.

Recently, we were given a classic demonstration of this cultural phenomenon. Every day, the bar and restaurant at Brennillis serves hundreds of superb lunches. It was towards the end of the lunchtime session and my wife was feeling hungry, so I asked if there was any cake to go with our coffee. The owner - normally a kindly and affable man - looked as if I had asked if he would like to buy some dirty pictures of his wife, and said rather curtly that there was no cake available. A few minutes later, a lady customer emerged from the restaurant area to pay her bill. As we left, the owner asked pointedly if Madame had enjoyed her cake. He did not add that she had eaten it for dessert in the proper place at the proper time, but what he meant was clear. Things are changing even in *France profunde*, but it is good to see some old habits dying so hard.

Mur-de-Bretagne

With its nose-in-the-air attitude, Mur-de-Bretagne looks out of place in the most down-to-earth county of Brittany. Although solidly built there is an ineffable air of upmarketness about the town which reminds me of a twee village in the Cotswolds. Contributing to this air of comfortable middle-classness is a very good English bookshop and coffee house in the shadow of the church, where the owner is still recovering from our request for a cup of coffee of the instant variety.

There is an evening market at Mur during the summer months, with the expected top-end comestibles on sale around the square and most of the shops staying open more than usually late. A mixture of pop and traditional Breton music comes from local bands, and the end of the season is marked by a grand *grillade* barbecue. Another suitably trendy feature of Mur is that the tower of the church is used to teach abseiling.

Further along the edge of the great lake is the village of Caurel, where there is a very well-stocked and satisfyingly old-fashioned English grocery store. It is very popular with British expatriates, though some are said to pick their orders up under the cover of darkness. It has long puzzled and irritated me how Britons living abroad are supposed to give up their favourite foodstuffs for fear of ridicule and condemnation by the chattering classes. The same people actively encourage settlers in Britain to pursue the traditions and preferences of their home country, and would be horrified at the thought of a French person living in England developing a taste for sliced white bread and Marmite. But the idea of a British expat seeking out proper baked beans and peanut butter spread is for some reason viewed with contempt and even horror by those who like to tell us what we should eat and drink as well as what we should think.

Pontivy

Like other mid-range Breton towns, I think Pontivy would be a pleasant place to live if you were old or young. It is big enough to have all the facilities you need at each end of the age spectrum and the town has a comfortably refined but non-snotty feel about it. This is probably down to the quality and tone of the ancient buildings and modern shops ranged around the medieval walkways. A huge bonus to Pontivy's appeal is that it sits on a confluence of canal and riverways and boasts a really classy fortified *château*. As any tourist knows, there are castles and castles, but the one at Pontivy is the real deal and looks and feels as if it means business. Work started on the fortress in the 17th century at the behest of one of the great Lords of Rohan. I cannot report if the inside matches the exterior, as on the day we called it was shut for lunch. A minute before two o' clock I followed a pretty young woman through the small door beside the great gates, but found myself in the staff toilets rather than the courtyard.

Leaving Pontivy we passed through Loudéac, and, by and large, that seems to us to be the best thing to do.

For absolutely no good reason, we find this central Côtes d'Armor town depressive and oppressive. It might be that our two visits were on a bad day for the town or us, but on the first occasion we were so menaced by a group of drunken yobs that we felt we had been teleported back to Britain. The next time we got much less than a warm welcome in a bar, and saw not a single Loudéacan smile during our time there. As all restaurateurs quickly learn, one bad experience is all it takes to put a visitor off. This should not apply to a whole town and we will give Loudéac a third chance, but not in the near future. For those who want to see how wrong I have it, there are five major horseracing events each year and a considerable forest near to hand to explore. Each Easter the *Palais de Congress et Culture* is transformed into Jerusalem for the Passion of Loudéac, so someone obviously feels strongly positive about the town.

Wednesday 14th

There is often something about the eyes of survivors of wars or tragedies. Whether they want to or not, they still must look back and recall the horrors. This preoccupied and even haunted look is also found on the faces of some Britons who have decided to run a pub or restaurant in France. Sometimes they also wear the expression of someone who has just realised it is not a good idea to put your hand in a chip pan to see if the oil is boiling yet.

Of all strange and inexplicable compulsions, taking on a pub or eating-place abroad seems right up there with self-mutilation. Who in their right mind would come up with the idea of starting a business in which they had absolutely no experience, and in a foreign land to boot? Then there is the slight handicap of not speaking the language, and the fact that pubs and restaurants head the bankruptcy lists of French enterprises when run by French people, let alone foreigners. There is a saying amongst embittered Britons who have set up shop in France that the best way to make a small fortune in this country is to start with a large one, and nowhere is this more apt or applicable than when trying to make a go of a bar or restaurant here or in any foreign land.

My wife and I know what the true cost of running a pub on either side of the Channel can be, and Donella is under strict instructions to hit me very hard with the nearest blunt instrument if I even mention the idea of taking on another licensed business. But, as I said to her this morning while she eyed a nearby lump hammer, it does no harm to look, and we owe a duty to my readers to consider all sorts of businesses taken on by Brits in Brittany.

The pub for sale is in a village remote even by rural Brittany standards, and comes complete with spacious accommodation, a large garden, several spectacularly distressed barns, a grocery shop and the garage and service station next door. Behind the workshop is a former ballroom still equipped with mirrored glitterball, and allegedly used by the French Resistance for covert meetings during the Second World War. Another intriguing piece of information not included in the property information details but passed on by the current owner is that a number of German officers went out of the back door of the ballroom with pretty local girls and never returned. The all-in asking price for all the properties and potential businesses is less than a hundred thousand Euros. The proprietor is a down-to-earth Scot who had run successful country pubs in England. Over a beer he told us candidly that when he took the place over he could just about get by on the twenty regular customers the bar attracted. In the last three years, several of his thirstiest punters had died, and with it his bar business. All the motorists in the village went to the local supermarket for cheap petrol, and as his wife refused to learn how to be a motor mechanic at 68, he could offer no other services at the service station.

Saturday 24th

Anglo-Info is a very popular website franchise which provides information and contacts for those Brits wishing to move to or buy property in different regions of France. The Brittany version is particularly well-run and useful, though you might not want to share a cab with many of the regular forum users. Like most on-line clubrooms, this part of the site is dominated by a sometimes breathtakingly opinionated clique. Most of them have obviously learned to type but not to think. To enter the forum on most of these sites is akin to pushing open the door of an unfamiliar village pub and hear silence descend as the debating society at the bar turn to look down their noses at you, the intruder. The irony is that as well as being contemptuous of visitors, the members of these cabals seem to dislike each other and their opinions even more.

Asking a simple question about how to register a British

car in France will result in a dozen contradictory replies before the senders abandon the point of the exercise and descend into a verbal punch-up

There are, however, pearls to be found in the accounts of those expats or holiday home owners who have fallen foul of an ordnance from the make-it-up-as-we-go-along department of their local town hall. This morning I came across a corker from a bemused Brit who related how, some years before, he and his wife had applied for permission to erect a shed in their back garden in Morbihan. The okay was duly given, and the couple got as far as laying the concrete base before being distracted by other more pressing matters. Recently, they decided to finish the job off, and anxious to go by the letter of the law, contacted the town hall to ensure all was well with their intentions. Back came the reply that the couple could not in fact put the shed on the concrete base, as their garden had been declared a nature reserve.

*   *   *

We have set a first by weeding a stretch of water.

According to our landlady, the previous owner drained the big pond to claim his fish before leaving. Grass seeds had taken root before it was re-filled, and, now the growing season has begun, it looks like a neglected paddy-field.

After hearing the owner's cautionary tales about the muddy depths and finding a single Wellington boot rooted in the shallows, we tried a number of solutions. An improvised raft sank before I got aboard, and a pair of garden shears tied to a broomstick proved unsatisfactory as a long-distance pruner. After much practice, we found a garden rake with a length of rope tied to the handle did the trick. It was inevitable that our nearest neighbour would appear just as I was casting the device at a dense patch of zoysia grass by the inlet channel. After watching me haul in the line and untangle my catch from the tines of the rake, he shook his head, adjusted his cap and went off to tell the other residents of Lesmenez about the curious manner in which the English like to fish.

Monday 26th

Our village now has its own Rites of Spring celebration, and I am the unintentional creator.

I don't know who counted them or how, but impeccable sources have it that there are around a ton of earthworms for every acre of soil in Britain. Each year they pass ten tons of soil through their bodies, though the report does not say if that is in total or each.

Aristotle described them as the intestines of the earth, and Darwin thought that few creatures had played such an important part in the history of our planet as the lowly earthworm. As well as being amazingly industrious, the earthworm can put an ant to shame for feats of strength, and can shift stones up to sixty times its own weight.

This may be so, but it would be some sort of earthworm which could take on the granite rocks lying just below the surface in this part of Brittany. I dug up at least sixty times my bodyweight to make our vegetable patch, and this may be the reason that the chicken compound seems to be a no-go area for worms. Yesterday evening I tried an old fishermen's trick by laying a sheet of plywood on the ground and jumping up and down on it. Worms, like moles, are said to be attracted by vibration and sound, so I accompanied my foot stamping with a burst of *Walking the Dog* on my blues harmonica.

It was of course inevitable that our nearest neighbour would arrive to see what was going on, and equally inevitable that he would show me the proper Breton way to jump up and down. Our combined efforts attracted our part-time neighbour and Parisian Mr Vitre, who despatched his wife to fetch a bottle of wine and alert the rest of the village that there was a party going on. An hour later and the home-made cider and bootleg apple brandy was flowing, we had been joined by the Breton bagpiper and Lesmenez was staging its first Fest Noz.

Dancing Lessons:

For those not familiar with the event, a Fest Noz ('Festival of the Night') is a sort of barn dance without the barn. And often without the dancing, come to that. The tradition dates back to at least the Middle Ages, and its origins and purpose are unclear. Mind you, given the amount of drink that is consumed at these bashes, that is not surprising. Officially, it is thought that the event was to mark and celebrate the completion of a new house. The owners would invite their neighbours to a shindig as a thank-you for their help on the building, and also to act as a sort of mass human steamroller. When everyone had drowned their inhibitions with copious draughts of home-brew firewater, it was time for the ceremonial Fest Noz dance. This was quite literally a knees-up, with no formal steps or intentions other than jumping up and down a lot on the spot. The crafty part was that as well as being good fun, the repeated impact of several dozen pairs of clog-clad feet on the earth floor made it instantly fit for purpose.

To spur the guests on to (literally) greater heights in this ancient forerunner of punk pogo-dancing, everyone was supplied with unlimited quantities of chouchenn. What Ancient Brits probably knew as mead, this innocuous-sounding but lethal infusion is basically fermented honey and water. Sometimes the brew was livened up with cider, and often with the corpses of the bees themselves to add to the texture and taste. The result was an interesting concoction which weighed in at (at least) 14 percent alcohol by volume.

When you think that the average beer or cider would be around 4-5 percent strength, you can see how a pint or two would encourage the guests to jump about with some abandon. Having tasted the stuff, I reckon it also had another valuable function. Any leftovers could be thinned down a bit and used as glue to waterproof the roof of the new building.

Made in the USA
Monee, IL
12 June 2024

59815018R10128